FRENCH
By Design

FRENCH
By Design

BETTY LOU PHILLIPS

GIBBS·SMITH
PUBLISHER

SALT LAKE CITY

ENDSHEETS: *A sampling of Peter Fasano Wallcovering, Great Barrington, Massachusetts.*
PRECEDING OVERLEAF: *With Gothic revival styling and a hand-forged iron railing encircling the terrace, luxury resides in the details of this architectural masterpiece that captures the essence of America. It could, however, just as well overlook the upscale fishing village of St.-Jean-Cap-Ferrat, settled long before America was born. The interior unites imposing eighteenth-century pieces from diverse places—most persuasive proof of the glory of France.* THIS PAGE: *With vintage fabrics and furniture, this old-fashioned sunporch charms the family year-round. Low-maintenance dove grey slate readily handles paw prints and spills. Under a collection of old ceiling canopies sits a settee; its light weight means it can easily be carried outside in nicer weather.* CONTENTS PAGE: *A Louis XV antique fountain sculpted in France has found a* bonne adresse *in the States, where it gives rise to gracious living as Americans savor its old-world splendor. Although it may once have been anxious about the future, today its arched jets splash proudly into a beautiful pool.*

Second Edition
04 03 02 01   7 6 5

Published by
Gibbs Smith, Publisher
P.O. Box 667
Layton, UT 84041

Orders (1-800) 748-5439
Visit our Web site at www.gibbs-smith.com

Designed by Traci O'Very Covey
Edited by Gail Yngve
Printed and bound in Hong Kong

Library of Congress Cataloging-in-Publication Data

Phillips, Betty Lou
French by design / Betty Lou Phillips.—1st ed.
p. cm.
ISBN 0-87905-972-9
1. Interior decoration —United States—History—20th century.
2. Decoration and ornament, Rustic—France—Influence. I. Title

NK2004.P54 2000
747.24—dc21   00-029148

"*Every man has two
nations, and one of
them is France.*"

—Benjamin Franklin

CONTENTS

I am grateful to the designers who allowed us to photograph their work, including Susan Arnold, Deborah Fain, Beverly Heil, Patricia Herrington, Rebecca Hughes, Thomas Manche, Joseph Minton, Christina Phillips, Kelly Phillips, Marilyn Phillips, and Richard Trimble.

Thank you, too, to the home owners who permitted us behind otherwise closed doors, where we could enjoy their gracious interiors, beautiful outdoor settings, and magnificent views, including Carol and Steve Aaron, Susan and Jack Arnold, Carolyn and Douglas Bailey, Barbara and Barry Beracha, Patricia and Gilbert Besing, Beverly and Terry Heil, Lou Kadane, Dorothy and David Kennington, Mary Lois and Sloane Leonard, Stacye and Michael McIntyre, Joseph Minton, Kelly and Brian Phillips, Christina and Bryce Phillips, Virginia Self Rainer, Sandra and Tom Rouse, and more.

A special thank you to those friends who kindly gave their time and energy, or offered an introduction or an idea, especially Pamela Anderson, Michael Bahr, P. J. Bergin, Judy Blackman, Carole Lou Bruton, Donna Burley, Nancy Caperton, Susan Lind Chastain, Bruno de la Croix-Vaubois, Sara Demartini, Annette Etcheverry, Harold Hand, Ross Iver, Jolie Jelacic, Nana Kay Kersh, Liz Lank, Joe Lugo, Kathleen Neely, Ginny Parker, Kelly Phillips, Lee Mahood, Kay McCloud, Jane Pierce, Carrie Ryan, Stacye Sapp, Patricia Schanbaum, Marilyn Smith, Cheryl Soto, Jayne Taylor, Mike Williams, Patricia Wood, and Warren Wyatt.

I am also highly indebted to architect Don Schieferecke, who so generously shared both his time and knowledge, and architects Kurt Segerberg and Richard Drummond Davis for sharing their enthusiasm for this project.

Instrumental in meeting this deadline were Rodney Tweet, Art Baker, Rex Brown, Max Brun, Harold Clayton, David Ferrand, Jerry Gates, Jeffrey Jauquet, Frank Martinez, Philip Minton, Kevin Ryan, Tim Ryan, Albert Sisneros, and Dennis Thompson as well as Ruby Medina, Mary Rodriguez, Cynthia Hollingsworth, Donna Sisneros, Helen Romero, and Gloria Gonzales.

A hôtel particulier (private residence or mansion in the city) invites visitors back to eighteenth-century France. Designed for gracious living, interior spaces brim with deep limestone fireplaces, timber-beamed ceilings, weathered walls, and rich hardwood floors. French doors open to lush plantings and a Louis XV fountain.

I have true admiration and appreciation for the talented photographers with whom I worked: Emily Minton, Dan Piassick and Nancy Edwards, and Tom Owens.

French by Design is also the result of the efforts of editor Gail Yngve and book designer Traci O'Very Covey, whose creativity and talents helped shape this book as well as *Provençal Interiors: French Country Style in America*.

Finally, thank you to my husband, John Roach, and the family who brightens our lives. Without their cooperation, this project would not be.

INTRODUCTION

"Beauty hath

strange power."

—JOHN MILTON

Much ado has been made about the sheer artistry of the French. In this capricious world, they are keepers of an inimitable style and way of life that will not surrender to modern influences. Rather, eras connect, seamlessly embracing not only what is but also what has been. Plainly, the French have a talent for successfully pairing fragments long associated with their country's past in a manner befitting the present. ❧ The rich simplicity of settings starts with furnishings handed down from generous great-aunts, great-uncles, and grandparents. As rooms take shape, they pick up even more threads of history. French people spend a lifetime leisurely combing their country, documenting yesterdays, carving out a private world where warmth and comfort are integrated

PRECEDING OVERLEAF: *An unseen groin-vaulted ceiling reminiscent of Gothic architecture sets this entry apart, while fine antiques hinting at the beauty beyond invite the eye to new discoveries.* OPPOSITE: *An important eighteenth-century Louis XV armoire—made of walnut and including its original hardware—serves as an entry closet. It was found in the historic city of Arles, where van Gogh painted* Starry Night *and more than two hundred other canvases. Although Americans often coyly hide their televisions behind closed armoire doors, much of France is appalled by the idea.*

in their own way. Without fail, a passion for France and a love of family and one another guide them. ❧ So it follows that seemingly everywhere one looks there are bountiful bouquets, treasured

books, photographs of family and friends, scented candles, and tabletop antiques reflecting the interests, travels, and pursuits of the occupants. Handsomely carved marriage armoires, towering *vaisseliers* (hutches), and *enfilades* (buffets with three or more doors) of grand proportions serve as the backdrop for *fauteuils* (armchairs), tables, and *tabourets* (footstools) with a patina of age.

Kitchens are the social epicenters, offering havens for families. *Objets de cuisine*—pots and utensils that are dear to the French—exemplify their dedication to masterfully preparing and artistically presenting meals.

More often than not, floors are bare, although some wear humble sea grass or bordered sisal. Also, faded oriental rugs and Aubussons, which take their name and inspiration from the French city where they were made, evoke an antique air.

Time-honored textiles—borrowed from eighteenth- and nineteenth-century pattern books—abound. Unassuming lengths of cottons, linens, and silks affectionately hug beds, walls, upholstery, and tables, linking rooms effortlessly with their palettes. Window treatments often puddle on the floor, with simple braid or luxurious fringe subtly highlighting the difference between modest and elegant. Artful details such as smocking, shirring, or pencil-thin piped edging also bring a stylish touch to richly textured rooms.

The enduring appeal of French country spans the centuries, bonding nobility and common folk, who eagerly put their imprint on a way of life that mingles elegance and ease. After years of largely echoing the furniture, fabrics, and accessories linked with the region of Provence, these days French country is often far removed from the primitive rough-hewn finishes that hearken back to the early seventeenth century and the picturesque countryside.

To be sure, French country has dressed itself up since

Louis XIII ascended the throne in 1610. Setting it apart now and forever is a kaleidoscope of styles reflecting various influences and periods, with furnishings most often drawn

Beckoning visitors into a kitchen is a pleasing mix of French and Italian influences that not only bridges the gap between two cultures but also retraces the past. A center island offers extra workspace for serious cooks whose inventive cuisine transcends international boundaries.

Transcending casual European living, shapely chairs are covered in Bennison Oakleaf with the selvage used for flanging. Adorning the sofa is Bennison's Centenary, woven in England, quilted, then edged in a complementary Peter Fasano check. A custom West Coast Trimming embellishes the throws. All fabrics were custom colored, too. The Buccellati oak-leaf dish was a gift from house-guests. Photographs chronicle the comings and goings of family members much like an album.

With Louis XVI retrofitted oak paneling, Régence globes, and a scholarly air, this library provides the perfect setting for reading, working, or visiting with friends.

Like a painting, eighteenth-century Portuguese tiles receive nods of approval, delivering a posh finishing touch to a gathering place off the kitchen.

TRANSCENDING TIME ZONES AND CONNECTING CULTURES, FRENCH COUNTRY STRIKES THE PERFECT CHORD.

from the reign of Louis XV or a blur of Louis styles that complement each other.

History aside, its charm lies in its versatility. Transcending time zones and connecting cultures, French country strikes the perfect chord. Relaxed yet refined and steeped in ways of life long past, sophisticated early pieces mix easily with the comforts of the twenty-first century, bringing understated luxury to rooms that escape the *ormolu* (faux gold leaf) or gilt of more formal French spaces.

In truth, patrons don't seem to mind that French country has become a catchall term for a style that was once known as French Provincial. It later became French country—when Pierre Moulin and his partner Pierre LeVec opened the first of twenty-two Pierre Deux shops around the world—and over time has become Provençal country. Still, whether right or wrong, much of the time, Americans refer to rooms filled with Louis furniture as French country.

Appropriately, we find the sheer beauty of France an ongoing feast for our admiring gaze—its eventful history, glamorous culture, and heightened sophistication, forever fascinating. As if this weren't enough, we focus on the attitudes of the French, looking to them for clues about how we should be living, cooking, decorating. For nowhere is a keen appreciation for all things French stronger than among Americans.

With this in mind, we invite you to join us as we salute the tapestry we know as France, along with the exhilarating style of her people—their venerable artistry, their attention to detail, their influence in the design world, and mostly, their influence on us. In *French by Design,* American designers exalt the splendors of France, the birthplace of our inspiration.

BETTY LOU PHILLIPS, ASID

HENRY LAHIRE
ARCHITECTE
1913

6 B.

ARCHITECTURAL
PRESENCE

*"Fine art is that
in which the hand,
the head and the heart
of man go together."*

—JOHN RUSKIN

In mosaic France, there are as many kinds of houses as there are regions. Set in a peaceful Breton fishing village, hidden in the orchards of Normandy, tucked deep in a valley protected by the towering Alps, or perched on a rocky harbor of the Côte d' Azur, dwellings differ markedly in architecture and character from one region to another. *Départements,* which are the French equivalents of our states, all have their own attributes, and are often named after the main river splicing through them. It is to the eighteenth- and nineteenth-century country craftsmen in each area that we owe this diversity. Architecture — like local customs and cuisine — is deeply rooted in tradition and has been long influenced by the climate, terrain, and available building materials. Whether a

PRECEDING OVERLEAF: *The imposing ornamentation above this door was carved in the twentieth century.* OPPOSITE: *Life in America may differ from that in France, but this impressive dwelling brings to mind how seamlessly the world of the French and our world are intertwined.*

vine-covered *château* (castle), a stately manor house called a *bastide,* or a *hôtel particulier* (the private mansion with wisteria spilling over its courtyard walls), each symbolizes a unique way of life. Also,

proudly bearing the country's storied past is the small stone farmhouse, or *mas*—the typical dwelling, with an unassuming spirit, ringed by lavender fields in Provence.

Humble or grand, a French house has allure. But the key to its cachet lies in its relationship to surrounding properties. When the scale of a dwelling is in harmony with neighboring spaces and the site on which it stands, no other style so captivates the imagination or compels interpretation half a world away.

Ultimately, though, it is the bounty of architectural assets—imposing arches, tall windows, and generous moldings—that bestow distinction on even the most masterful mix of building materials and intricate craftsmanship. Stripped of all furnishings, the most breathtaking homes resound with detailing that permits each to make a dramatic statement on its own.

In citified France, behind iron gates and towering walls that hide a tangle of tales, handsome heavy doors exude noble airs with a mélange of dates, inscriptions, and family crests etched overhead or cut deep into the stone. Practiced, too, at emitting aristocratic attitudes are the oversized hinges straining valiantly, lending unshakable support to the well-worn bolts and locks authoritatively guarding entrances. Only the inviting courtyards and the broad stone steps leading to the knockers on groaning doors hint that those who care to visit will be met with courtesy and unfolding charm.

Towering windows and ceiling-high glass doors welcome splashes of light and the sounds of the day. Set with appealing symmetry, they open wide onto balconies with impressive views of lushly landscaped gardens and ancient chestnut trees. At the beginning

Exuding the style of a country house that has high ceilings and proportionally tall arched doors, these walls look convincingly old. The antique lighting fixture is from Ainsworth-Noah, the largest showroom in the Atlanta Decorative Arts Center. A library is seen through this doorway.

STRIPPED OF ALL FURNISHINGS, THE MOST BREATHTAKING HOMES RESOUND WITH DETAILING THAT PERMITS EACH TO MAKE A DRAMATIC STATEMENT ON ITS OWN.

An aged-looking baroque design draws the eye to a master bedroom ceiling where it unites the room's quiet palette without competing with the architecture. The curtain fabric is from Marvic and the chandelier from Niermann Weeks.

of the twentieth century, surface bolts and *crémone* bolts (locking mechanisms) became *de rigueur* hardware on windows in households throughout France, where the mellowness of brushed nickel, steel, and pewter has quelled most thoughts of brass.

Crisp crown moldings, seamlessly woven together and as carefully constructed as couture dresses or tailor-made suits, serve as the wardrobes for rooms. Fittingly, they are dressed in the period during which the home was built, before step-ping out onto ceilings, making spaces appear even taller than they actually are. Calling attention to the French intuitive sense of scale and proportion, these sophisticated ensembles deftly lace their way through meandering spaces where scented candles flicker and fireplaces glow.

In the classic company of seductively lit chandeliers shimmering in large antique mirrors, guests show passing interest in the rich trims framing windows, nod to the tapestries and heroic-sized portraits hanging three high on hand-

Crossing the elegant threshold is much like entering an eighteenth-century French château with an engraved invitation to study art history. After admiring the limestone fireplace from another era and marveling at the antique candlesticks casting a warm glow, one may climb the wide stone stairs and examine the ancient tapestry hanging among the splendor. Follow, too, the strains of "Clair de Lune" wafting from an antique Steinway piano with ivory keys. It graces the music room that looks down on the foyer.

finished plaster walls, and focus on antiques that have furnished the house for centuries.

But it is the wide curving staircases—flowing in the direction that allows a person bravely defending the stairs to freely swing his sword arm clockwise—that most captures attention. Models for the world to admire, each is a sophisticated work of art with exquisitely fashioned ironwork, as might be expected, since the French have long been renowned for their skill in making magnificent objects from iron.

In this era of mass production, the French remain masters at creating hand-forged fluid pieces with unmistakable flair. Preserving an architectural tradition with roots in fourteenth-century Europe while remaining faithful to family tradition, gifted hands—lured by the malleability of the metal—pass exacting old-world techniques their fathers and grandfathers taught them from generation to generation.

Summing up all that is French, graceful eighteenth-century gates protect a maison de maître, *or master's house, that is adjacent to a courtyard.*

An exterior staircase tucked into this French Renaissance structure leads to a network of bedrooms and hallways.

An eighteenth-century loveseat with Pierre Frey moiré check has a place of honor beneath a prized Belle Époque painting. Poised on the marble-topped table is a vintage teapot salvaged from a grand hotel in Europe during the 1920s or 1930s. Steeped in charm and designed for heavy use, sturdily plated commercial serving pieces and flatware—known as Hôtel *silver—were produced for restaurants, railways, ships, and hotels. If looking to start a collection, set off for the Village Saint-Paul in Paris's fourth* arrondissement. *It is unlikely, however, that the Hollohaza hand-decorated chocolate pots from Hungary can be found on the Avenue du Paradis, the street where Parisians and tourists alike buy Limoges porcelain off the shelf.*

THE BEAUTY
OF NATURE

❦

*"What I love is near
at hand. Always in
earth and air."*

—THEODORE ROETHKE

For thousands of years, houses in France have reflected a regional identity, creating a rambling gallery of architectural history. Drawn to the earth's resources strewn nearby and using local materials, the French built modest stone dwellings, unpretentious timber-framed houses, and elegant châteaux, each home with its own color palette and texture. During the nineteenth century, limestone gathered in nearby fields or quarried locally was the most coveted stone for urban homes, partly because of its simple elegance, mostly because it could be carved and cut without splitting. However, in some construction, different-shaped and -sized rough stones with worn edges, known as *moellons,* or rubble stones, were used in their original state. In keeping with the grandeur of other homes, masons cut, shaped, or carved the limestone with a mallet and chisel into rectangular blocks, then set about building structures that would last beyond

PRECEDING OVERLEAF: *An abundance of charming postcard-perfect homes captures the allure of France. Here, climbing roses blanket a facade worn by time.* OPPOSITE: *Guided by the spirit of eighteenth-century France, a maison de campagne, or country house, built a year ago proudly follows the contours of the land on which it stands. Towering over the village below, it takes its cue from nature's rich resources, linking stone, iron, copper, and sand. It also boasts the characteristically thick walls of homes dotting the French Alps that keep dwellings cool in summer.*

ABOVE: *Colorful potted geraniums line a limestone stairway in Provence.* OPPOSITE: *A suitably grand door with magnificent hardware opens to a thought-fully appointed entry where torchieres light the way to a series of welcoming rooms. Smooth stones called "quoins" edge the doorway.*

the masons' lifetimes. Dressed stone *(pierre de taille)* worked into desired shapes was saved for the decorative quoins that reinforced corners, framed windows, and doors.

Some of the finest limestone was found on the French plain outside Caen in the Lower Normandy region, where large quantities of granite, sandstone, and schist (a naturally layered rock) were also located. In nearby Brittany, situated in the northwestern corner of France, which juts boldly into

the Atlantic, sturdy granite houses were built among half-timbered ones. *Basalt,* a black volcanic stone nearly as hard as granite, was common to Auvergne, at the heart of the Massif Central region, while Roussard stone, the most attractive of all sandstones, was widespread in the Mayenne and western Corrèze regions.

In areas where stone was not to be had, pebbles were often garnered from riverbeds then set in mortar to form walls.

A peninsula in this Provençal waterway makes an attractive garden.

A well-tended rose arbor creates a fragrant cover for this private pathway.

FRENCH LESSONS

*"When love
and skill work
together, expect a
masterpiece."*
—JOHN RUSKIN

On this side of the Atlantic, a mix of scattered dwellings evocative of old-world France snugly fit the passions of their owners. Down tangled streets, elegant masonry, steeply gabled slate roofs, and dormers with *oeils-de-boeuf* (bull's-eye windows) seep into pricey new construction alongside European-inspired estates developed earlier. ❧ Affection for France travels into dining rooms fit for honoring its president, brick-walled caves where wine is stored at 55 degrees with 70-percent humidity, and chefs' kitchens with cabinets made from 200-year-old cherry trees cut from the Fontainebleau forest outside Paris. Dwellings with newly acquired French overtones, rising majestically across America, should not be compared, however, to chateaux that have withstood the test of time in the sprawling French countryside. ❧ Granted, some exteriors conform to exacting French standards, with stone fences and swimming

PRECEDING OVERLEAF: *With its imposing regal presence and overpowering beauty, this splendid Louis XV French Renaissance chateau stands neither cracked nor crumbled by time. But, then, it is not the typical dwelling that one sees outside a hundred French towns on the standard road trip from Paris to the Riviera. Rather, it is the ne plus ultra of chateaux and firmly planted on American soil.* OPPOSITE: *Brick walls, a trompe l'oeil mural, and an old iron chandelier frame an intimate tasting room laid with thick eighteenth-century ginger-colored paving stones transported from Europe. Teeming with admirable wines, inviting embossed leather chairs, and tapestry seating, the setting is as distinctive as each of Paris's twenty* arrondissements *and is ideal for leisurely sampling the finest of France's fare.*

pools that could pass for centuries-old ponds. Though, for the most part, interiors are clearly American, harmonious with our contemporary taste for family rooms, exercise rooms, and home offices—rooms that once did not exist but are as important to our lifestyles today as strong floor plans, plentiful light, and sweeping views. After all, in the United States, twenty-first-century life moves at a different pace.

As we inch onto increasingly congested highways and look for ways to shave crucial time off our daily schedules, trappings such as palatial bathrooms, surround-sound media rooms, his-and-her wardrobes, and laundry rooms on the bedroom level are cherished.

In urban trophy neighborhoods with top schools, prized trees, and proximity to city offices, some dwellings of modest origins with moody kitchens and small bathrooms have been razed. Others, whose facades reveal little of what lies within, expectantly wait to be torn down by enthusiastic new owners making way for residences that better fit the American dream as symbols of success. Meanwhile, handsome houses of varying heights that stand out from their neighbors await loving restoration by the dedicated and patient drawn to their French architecture.

In homage to this gallery of hipped-, gabled-, and mansard-roof styles, crowned with layers of slate, tile, and stone, it is only fitting that we strive for ideals that are indelibly French with, of course, an *au courant* edge.

Unfortunately, removing walls between rooms, turning a once-drab maid's quarters into a discreet spa, or other ambitious undertakings, such as raising ceilings, are seldom a smooth or simple process. All too often, underlying glitches add tension to works in progress, pushing the limits of tolerance.

The fairest of all antique mirrors, flanked by a pair of Paul Ferrante sconces wearing Jim Thompson shades, adorns this powder room with a stunning onyx sink. Sherle Wagner built its reputation for luxury in the 1940s by introducing 24-karat gold-plated fixtures like the onyx ones shown here.

If one's home is his or her castle, shouldn't the dining room seat sixteen, and shouldn't an army of Louis XV chairs guard a table set with china from Bernardaud's Versailles collection? After all, for more than a hundred years, from 1682 to 1789, Versailles was the seat of the royal court and the political capital of France. Impressive by day, this room becomes glamorous at night when golden light and dramatic shadows spring from the hand-carved stone fireplace, from the antique candlesticks holding court on the mantel, and from the chandeliers that once hung in a hotel in Avignon. Since commanding dining tables were not made until the era of Louis XVI, Old Timber Table Company in Dallas crafted the thirteen-foot walnut table from aged wood.

Taking its cue from sprawling Versailles, this oak flooring was cut on an angle before being laid in a classical pattern. Designs from the Petit Trianon, the Grand Trianon, and the Petit Hameau—set amid grounds of the Palace of Versailles—also run through this chateau, mirroring the past.

For those considering restoring an old house to some version of its former glory, here's help opening the door to French influences:

When it comes to adding twenty-first-century comforts without disturbing period features already in place, be prepared to do some careful research to ensure that the "bones" of the house—the moldings, doors, windows, floors—not only replicate the past but are in keeping with the home's vintage.

Restorations in France generally rely on early authenticated plans, documents, or paintings. Studying architectural details in photographs of French rooms can also provide inspiration, as can tracking down other houses designed by the original architect. Faux pas can be glaring, so one should

Twisting tradition, hand-carved shell motifs found at a French flea market are reinvented as wall hangings.

avoid a collage of influences. Consulting a sensitive architect can help safeguard the integrity of the structure and can be a worthy investment.

If adding on, aim for a seamless transition so it is impossible to tell where the existing house ends and the new structure begins. Nothing looks worse than a new roof that doesn't match the original one in style, pitch, and materials, unless it's mismatched window *mullions* (vertical strips that divide the panes) and *muntins* (wood strips that hold glass panes). Early windows were generally square or horizontal with two classic panels separated by stone or wooden mullions and six or eight panes.

Some grand homes incorporate marble; however, stone, tile, and wood are often more natural choices for flooring in

Applying the standards of the French, craftsmanship praiseworthy of France starts at the front door. OPPOSITE: *A hefty hood adds character and bespeaks good taste while an ample-sized stove is a French essential in a working kitchen. However, with the pick of the world crops readily accessible, it is easy to borrow liberally from other cuisines. Undisputedly, Izraël Izraël is the most remarkable grocery store in Paris.*

French-country homes. Consider stripping rather than sanding old wood floorboards. To avoid added tear, the French do not shave their floors before refinishing them.

Nowadays, you need not live around the corner from a quarry to find tile as inviting as France itself. Nor must you settle for anything less than reclaimed terra-cotta pavers with the subtle color and texture that hint at long-standing use. Shipped directly from France and Italy, a good selection of both old and new stone can be found on American soil.

Despite best intentions, it is difficult to give a house a sense of history and still bend with the times. Taking clues from existing elements will help forge the connection, as will staking claim to salvaged objects gleaned from divergent sources. But then, having a vision is one thing; relentlessly hunting down those iron gates with the aura of age, thick solid doors, and impressive hardware culled from France is another. Fortunately, the Internet has opened a global marketplace with a broad assortment of treasures that are comforting reminders of things past.

The drawback, naturally, is that on-line shopping cannot beat the satisfaction of seeing an antique for yourself. Not only is it difficult to tell much from a digital photograph, but it means taking a chance on unknowns such as condition, followed by worries about returning goods that are not the quality expected.

SHIPPED DIRECTLY FROM FRANCE AND ITALY, A GOOD SELECTION OF BOTH OLD AND NEW STONE CAN BE FOUND ON AMERICAN SOIL.

Define the use of each space. While considering a room's function, try rethinking the basic floor plan to determine if an area is better suited to another need. For example, two small bedrooms may become a grand guest quarters with a sitting area and luxurious bath. Sweeping, open spaces offer limitless possibilities and are perfect for serious entertaining. Small rooms, however, offer more intimacy.

Leave nothing to chance. The smallest elements can make a striking difference: the quality of the ironwork, a lighting fixture proportionate to the size of the room, or the extra care in selecting grout colors and making sure joints are kept tight. Samples of original moldings can be sent to millwork shops for replication. On the other hand, no two door-knobs must necessarily be the same.

When remodeling a bathroom, remember it is best to select slabs personally, since no two pieces of either marble or stone are alike. For an aged look, seek honed (smooth but less shiny than a polished finish) slabs. Since porous materials stain easily, be sure to seal them annually so they remain water-resistant.

Trowel on layers of texture to give walls age-old charm. Then aim for glazes resembling those found in Provence, keeping in mind the eighteenth-century penchant for vibrant colors. A carefully chosen palette can help ease stresses of the day as well as give cramped quarters the feeling of space, and

A desk fit for a poet and an oval-backed chair appropriate for royalty publicize the creations of some of Italy's foremost woodworkers, carvers, and decorative painters. Patina's furnishings have the same beauty and presence as the antiques that inspired them. It is no wonder that Ann and Waverly Graham, the founders of the Atlanta-based company, are heralded as the world's leading manufacturers of Venetian-inspired furnishings this side of the eighteenth century.

In the spirit of French living, the focus of this bedroom is, of course, the bed—in this case a Patina bed made in Italy. That's not to say the room isn't romantically appointed with fine linens, a billowing bed skirt, glazed walls, Aubusson rug, and an unseen iron-and-crystal chandelier with rich amber crystals circa 1840. Early French chandelier makers used rock crystal—a mineral with natural facets—rather than glass.

ABOVE: *Chic curtains hanging from iron rods add panache to any room.*
OPPOSITE: *Though this setting is every bit as charming as a farmhouse in Provence, as Ralph Waldo Emerson pointed out, "The ornament of the house are the friends who frequent it."*

A PASSION FOR OLD-WORLD CRAFTSMANSHIP IS ONE OF THE MANY TRAITS THAT RULE THE FRENCH, WHO ARE NOT ONLY NOTORIOUSLY HARD TO PLEASE BUT WHO EXPECT A LEVEL OF WORKMANSHIP THAT, MORE OFTEN THAN NOT, ONLY MONEY CAN BUY.

make a large room less imposing. Glazing jarring architectural elements the same color as their closest neighbor helps mask any awkwardness and diminishes their presence.

Before spending serious money, take comfort in the fact that many houses in France, even in the chateau-rich, regal Loire Valley, show obvious signs of age with flaking paint, stained bathroom sinks, cracked tile, and unevenly worn floors that creak underfoot.

Of course, leaking roofs, inadequate electrical wiring, and primitive plumbing need replacing before you begin decorating. Money is well spent on worthy windows. Also, crumbling stone steps leading to the front door can make any house look shabby.

Whether addressing gnawing problems or fulfilling pricey dreams, don't skimp on quality. A passion for old-world craftsmanship is one of the many traits that rule the French, who are not only notoriously hard to please but who expect a level of workmanship that, more often than not, only money can buy. Consequently, they do not even consider tackling decorative painting themselves, or performing other tasks requiring skills they do not possess. Famous for their stubborn insistence on quality, to them professional-looking results mean turning projects over to experts with well-honed skills. Facing potentially daunting costs of renovating an aging property, they wisely prioritize their battles, believing some things are better left undone rather than done poorly.

To restore any house to its early splendor requires more than a rich imagination. Few would argue that it can be done on a shoestring budget. In truth, there is no greater challenge than setting a realistic allowance. After all, history can carry quite a price.

ABOVE: *To capture French charm in grand style for a St. Louis show house, the designer featured Prussian blue, one of Napoleon's favorite colors; it projected the prestige of his rule.*

OPPOSITE: *An appreciation for the old, the unusual, the unexpected, and the unique ultimately led to this powder room that looks far from commonplace.*

PROVENCE

∞

*"Long live the sun,
which gives us such
beautiful color."*

—PAUL CÉZANNE

For decades on end, the people of Provence lived simply, often lodging alongside their animals under one roof while drawing their livelihoods from the land. Today this same *région* is awash in new villas with terra-cotta-tile roofs, and restored farmhouses stand amid the tumbledown barns gracing the sun-blessed countryside.

Seduced by the magical light, tourists swarm to the hotels, stroll through the marketplaces, and find their way to tempting sidewalk cafés where they chatter meaningfully about the history of southern France. Even as symbols of rural France fade, it is the spirit of the past that continues to exercise its influence, luring outsiders and preserving legacies. In this era of greater well-being, villagers remain true to their roots, clinging to their quiet way of life, honoring family traditions,

PRECEDING OVERLEAF: *Typically, just 25 percent of Parisians live in houses, while in smaller cities 75 percent of the people dwell in single-family homes within earshot of each other. In France—a country with more than sixty million people—plenty of vacant land is available, but tidy, compact villages are designed to prevent urban sprawl into valuable fertile land.* OPPOSITE: *While the number of wines may appear infinite, all originate from but a few dozen grape varieties.*

believing they can get ahead through hard work, and savoring simple pleasures such as *dining en famille.* Perhaps most significant of all,

Street markets brim with hand-picked vegetables, ripe fruit, and beautiful flowers as well as fish, meat, cheese, and pasta bound for various kitchens. Bouillabaisse, a regal stew made with fresh fish and vegetables, is a specialty of Provence. OPPOSITE: *Shutters shield most houses from the unrelenting, mid-day Provençal sun and offer protection against the wind by cosseting newly integrated windows, or* portes-fenêtres, *known as French doors. The high-flying republican Tricolore replaced the fleur-de-lis as the royal symbol of France after the revolution in 1789.*

the strong allegiance they feel for their piece of the world remains unchanged.

With the willingness to look back while leisurely Provençal life moves forward comes a sense of progress and pride. Still, it is the unassuming farmhouses with their exposed beams, stone fireplaces, and symphony of colors celebrating the land, sun, and sea that give Provence much of its charm.

As dogs loll in doorways and against richly textured walls, a tidy palette of breathtaking blues appear in a spectrum of shades, ranging from the cobalt blue that bathes the Mediterranean, to the pale blue of the cloudless Provençal sky, to the violet blue carpeting of lavender beds faded by the sun.

Heralding the influence of Vincent van Gogh, rooms revel in brilliant sunflower yellow and glorious poppy red, deeper scarlet and rich terra-cotta. Amid the shifting shades of leafy greens from Claude Monet's celebrated Giverny garden, the

With few, if any, windows on its north side, a mas *in need of updating loyally promises centuries-old protection against the fierce north wind known as* le mistral. *Cosmetic restorations require using natural pigments that change with the light and practicing age-old methods that purposely keep a facade from appearing too new, invariably reinforcing thoughts about the French need for the past to be ever present.*

stony grays found in nature glisten. Color also takes its cues from the grapevines, orchards, olive groves, and wheat fields, as well as a patchwork of crops, including eggplants, peaches, and plums. Finally, in a country entrenched in its fabled past, dozens of mellow old-world shades of ochre, sienna, and umber are among the natural pigments fancied.

Filling the salt-swept air is the scent of lavender. Endless rows of olive trees spray the area with shade. Geraniums, begonias, and petunias tumble down steps or spill from window boxes perched between weathered shutters, brightening the façades. Tall, elegant cypress trees frame entrances, a custom reportedly dating back to Roman times when they alerted soldiers to the location of water.

These days, golden light spills through much-loved windows, soaking up the sun that is central to the *région's* lore and lure. But it was not always so. Before modern heating, windows were small and scarce, designed to keep walls from reverberating and helping them to stand their ground against the stern, heedless *mistral* that whistles through the south of France.

Now with lace curtains fluttering in the windows, unglazed terra-cotta tiles sprawling on kitchen floors, and steep, narrow stairwells spiraling to spare rooms with glazed walls, Provence is *très chic*.

Yet, what sets the *région* apart is not its picture-book setting, enticing shops, or abundance of good restaurants.

Just inside salvaged doors that once graced a country home in France, a cut limestone floor merges several different shapes, grandly reminiscent of the palace in Fontainebleu. Throughout, furniture is mostly French in style and provenance; however, the settee alongside the stairs is English. Above it hang full-size renderings, called "cartoons," that once served as models for needlepoint seat cushions. Throw pillows were made from vintage fabrics and trims.

Rather, the gentle, easygoing, hospitable spirit of a warm welcoming culture makes the area nothing less than irresistible. Neighbors greet neighbors and look out for one another. In addition, not only do villagers respect each other, but they also value the tourists and those who are investing money in the area.

As the economy has thrived, many outsiders have found that the ultimate luxury is owning a country house in a tranquil Provençal hamlet, say in Eygalières, one of Provence's most charming villages.

With eleven million Parisians packed tightly in the metropolitan area, and most living in apartments—fewer than a quarter of them live in houses—it is not surprising that many crave more-open spaces as a getaway from the pressures of city life. It helps, of course, that workers each have five weeks annual paid vacation, which, in turn, also helps explain why the French reportedly own more second homes than any other people.

Fueled by this age of affluence, some fashionable Americans are also trading the traffic-clogged Montauk Highway to their vacation homes in the Hamptons on Long Island's east end for French rural roads lined with majestic trees. To them, a life in Avignon, founded in the sixth century as a port on the banks of the Rhône, is becoming more and more attractive.

Paving the way for those looking to renovate a *mas* is the nonprofit group Maisons Paysannes de France, 32 rue Pierre Semard, 75009 Paris. Dedicated to the preservation of old farmhouses, each *département* has an English-speaking representative who can readily offer helpful advice about local traditions and materials.

A seductive mix of vintage velvets, old buttons, and pretty trims from a variety of places infuses a pillow sham with a new attitude plus glamour that brightens the room.

For example, it might be pointed out that the *petite tomette* tiles of Aix are not appropriate in Saint-Rémy-de-Provence, where Beaucaire limestone or terra-cotta is more historically fitting.

AS THE ECONOMY HAS THRIVED, MANY OUTSIDERS HAVE FOUND THAT THE ULTIMATE LUXURY IS OWNING A COUNTRY HOUSE IN A TRANQUIL PROVENÇAL HAMLET, SAY IN EYGALIÈRES, ONE OF PROVENCE'S MOST CHARMING VILLAGES.

Growing up is fun in this haven any young miss would be happy to call her own. With an amicable mix of pretty fabrics and trim—from Osborne & Little, Nobilis, and Cowtan & Tout—and an extra Jane Keltner four-poster bed for sleepover friends, the setting is also ideal for studying, lounging, and talking on the phone.

COMMUNICATING STYLE

∾

"Style is a magic wand, and turns everything to gold that it touches."

—LOGAN PEARSALL SMITH

The French like to think that a sense of style is in their genes, that it runs in families. Perhaps this is true. If not, it may indeed be acquired in childhood when affection for the commonplace, the elegant, and the antique starts young as children learn to appreciate beautiful things. ❧ Behind most every door, after all, lies a certain je ne sais quoi, or indescribable gift, that parents feel a responsibility to pass on, giving their children an edge from the cradle onward, and spurring our sense of wonderment over and over again. Truth is, we are struck by the flair of the French, reflecting their identity, interests, and heritage. It not only captures our attention but also inspires us to channel our energies in its pursuit. Of course, style is easy to recognize. Defining it can be more challenging. ❧ So what, then, is style? It means different things to different people. In a lot of minds, style is an unerring instinct as well as a way of life that prizes quality and flows from a penchant

PRECEDING OVERLEAF: *A sophisticated mix of Louis XV and Louis XVI furnishings shape a salon with architectural presence to spare. Painting the room with further importance are an eighteenth-century mirror, an antique chandelier, and a landscape of dramatic fabrics. Though neither formality nor pretension is a way of life in this home, the French traditionally receive and entertain guests in* le salon.

Impressionist Claude Monet, born in 1840, lived in the charming village of Giverny, forty miles northwest of Paris, from 1883 until his death in 1926—first as a tenant burdened with debt, then as a prosperous homeowner who never tired of painting his gardens. Michel Monet, the artist's son, who did not have children, bequeathed both the house and gardens to the Institut de France in 1966. They are now open to the public after being painstakingly restored.

for detail. Others see it as the discreet expression of knowledge, sophistication, and culture—emanating from within and subtly revealing itself in unassuming ways of living, decorating, and entertaining. Still others—many others—believe it is a dash of imagination bound with old-world elegance that gives life to the past while bringing understated luxury to rooms.

Say what you like, style is not an easy thing to come by, which is no doubt the reason we look to the French, who seemingly exude it with ease.

PRECEDING OVERLEAF: *As befitting a chateau as the French home it graces, statuary and dramatic dense greenery invite guests to revel in the pleasures of trompe l'oeil, which tampers with perceptions. Fort Worth, Texas, artist Gregory Arth's delightful deception lures the eye into seeing what is not really there, though there is no doubt that silk, hand painted in Venice, has been inset on chairs.*

Doors covering a mechanical area are castoffs from France.

Indeed, neither social standing nor money offers any guarantee of style. It cannot be procured on the Internet, nor can it be had from an overnight delivery service or via fame. So the French, standard bearers of style *par excellence*, have become our passports to good taste, luring us with their air of superiority, famous reserve, and example. For them, turning heads is second nature, thanks to the lofty way their priorities are reflected in not only what they wear or the confident manner in which they move, but also in the careful way they present themselves to the world.

To be sure, there is the orderly, symmetrical way in which they plan their gardens, many of which boast soaring trees, gurgling stone fountains, endless flowers, and a supply of vegetables and herbs that help shape the day's menus. Then, too, there is the classical manner in which they cherish the past, opening the countless layers of history to interpretation—that is, by adding new ideas to the mix while assembling intriguing collections and crowding tables with antique objets d'art. Also, there is the noteworthy way paintings of merit are not only tastefully arranged as a group, but appropriately hung in frames that are mindful of both their size and the era in which they were painted, though few have withstood the ravages of time in their original frames.

Accordingly, homes are chicly rendered works of art, impressively composed but more intimate than most any work of art can ever be. Exuding a passion for beauty, an intuitive sense of scale, harmony of color, and expression of one's inner self, it is as though rooms are created from varying points of view, each highlighting one's distinct aesthetic sensibility while offering a window into one's soul.

TO BE SURE, THERE IS THE ORDERLY, SYMMETRICAL WAY IN WHICH THEY PLAN THEIR GARDENS, MANY OF WHICH BOAST SOARING TREES, GURGLING STONE FOUNTAINS, ENDLESS FLOWERS, AND A SUPPLY OF VEGETABLES AND HERBS THAT HELP SHAPE THE DAY'S MENUS.

Restoring peace of mind comes easily in the comfort of this sumptuous Summer Hill chaise covered in Christopher Norman's Bordeaux plaid. The book table is from Ironies in Berkeley, California; the hand-painted, striped wall covering is by Elizabeth Dow in Manhattan; the small vase filled with delicate ranunculus is Baccarat.

Why bother with searching for a passport and packing a trunk when it's easy to put cares to rest in the kind of plush overnight accommodations that one might expect to find at the Hôtel Plaza Athénée, Hôtel Ritz, or Hôtel de Crillion in Paris without the princely prices that accompany a stay? Reflecting the French spirit of relaxed living, nineteenth-century confit *pots, now lamps, sit beside an Ironies king-sized* lit de fer *(iron bed), luxuriously plumped with pillows. As yards of fabric spill, billow, and flow, all that is missing is the French chocolates that have not as yet been left on turned-down sheets. L'Univers des Anges Gourmands at 49, avenue de la Bourdonnais in Paris's seventh* arrondissement *calls itself a* fleuriste du chocolat, *perhaps because it sells the most decadent chocolate bouquets.*

Undeniably, there are no so-called rules. There is, however, the French way of decorating—with intelligence, awareness, and panache. Priding themselves on their creative differences, interiors vary widely, taking shape according to one's definition of style. But, seemingly, rooms have the same raison d'être, or reason for being. Exhibiting a reverence for the past, they illustrate the French way of life with its matchless mix of simplicity, elegance, and grace.

Wrapped in detail, old furnishings share space with the new and luxurious fabrics with more-textured ones. There is a subtle blend of the expensive and the less costly. Often, too, there is an unexpected element of surprise, adding energy and sparkle to the rooms of people notorious for taking themselves seriously. *Classic* interiors are at once meaningful, airy, and laced with the feeling of relaxed sophistication—the very traits that offer ample proof of taste.

But, then, the French do not have a monopoly on taste, freedom of expression, or uncanny decorating skills. Americans, too, can be adroit at creating remarkably beautiful, understated rooms, although the former claim that we lean toward the showier, brasher, and, above all, over-the-top settings, which they often malign as the worst sin of all.

Nothing suggests flamboyance in most American homes—not that there aren't touches of luxury. Often, we favor sensual, opulent fabrics. But, in fact, we also use unpretentious cottons, denims, chenilles, and wool felt for both upholstery and window treatments, plus earthy solids, modest ticking stripes, and unassuming prints, plaids, and checks. And, while we are not afraid of color and pattern, our settings are not only poised to be pleasing to the eye but also to exude comfort and to reflect our individuality. Creating a world unto itself—representative of France, Italy, and elsewhere mingling amicably—fulfills our need for self-satisfaction perhaps even more than it does for our European counterparts.

To be sure, we do not want to be held hostage by a set of mandatory decorating rules or even be frightened off by formulas. Dreamers that we are, with a few suggestions to guide us, we typically insist on scripting our own spaces, trusting our own artistry, and expressing without apology our individuality in uniquely American ways while admittedly relying on the French for inspiration.

Although we let the French establish the standard of beauty by which our rooms are often judged and credit them for shaping the stylistic world we live in, we pride ourselves on juxtaposing colors, fabrics, and textures in our own way, and on being respected for our accomplishments.

We long for our baths to be calm retreats from the rough-and-tumble world and reminiscent of our respites at the best luxury hotels, where leisure has been treasured among whirlpool tubs, heated towel rails, and gleaming European fittings. Separate showers with large showerheads quiet the mind, soothe the senses, and befriend the spirit in satisfying doses. In short, we long for our bathroom to look just like the one pictured here with the subtle niceties of Bulgari soaps, a Peacock Alley sumptuous robe, and plump Pratesi towels from the renowned linen house.

CREATING A WORLD UNTO ITSELF—REPRESENTATIVE OF FRANCE, ITALY, AND ELSEWHERE MINGLING AMICABLY—FULFILLS OUR NEED FOR SELF-SATISFACTION PERHAPS EVEN MORE THAN IT DOES FOR OUR EUROPEAN COUNTERPARTS.

In a charming room awash with French influences, mealtime unfolds around a rectangular table with a carved apron, offering family-style seating, or what the French call a *table d'hôte. Like the fireplaces in chic European homes, the Louis XV one shown here has an impressive mantel and surround.*

At the far end of a great room sits a rare eighteenth-century walnut commode. Jacqueline Adams Antiques of Atlanta stumbled upon it in Romans, a French village near bustling Grenoble, where Protestant carvers favored carved wooden handles rather than adorning works with brass or bronze. To this day the eighteenth century is thought the most glorious era in European history, with society taking its cue from the courts of Versailles, Vienna, St. Petersburg, London, Potsdam, Turin, and more. The lamp with a French influence is from Panache in Los Angeles, the handmade shade from Bella Copia in San Francisco.
OPPOSITE: Since the fourteenth century, Europeans have coveted noble hand-woven tapestries. If the stories that abound are to be believed, weavers wandered from place to place, settling temporarily in the chateau, church, or monastery where they received a commission after presenting detailed drawings or paintings, often full-scale, called "cartoons." From these, they would copy chosen patterns. Nearby sits a table for reading or playing cards.

ADOPTING A FRENCH STYLE

*"The days come and go . . .
but they say nothing,
and if we do not use the gifts
they bring, they
carry them silently away."*
—RALPH WALDO EMERSON

The many facets of French style have long fascinated Americans. It is the seemingly effortless French way with design, flair for living well, and lingering respect for heritage, history, and quality that not only captures our interest but also makes the French so French.

   Yet, truth be told, one need not set foot on French soil to adopt *le style français* — though if one does, all the better, naturally. There is joy in wandering through the more than 300 antiques shops in L'Isle-sur-la-Sorgue, the perfume center of Grasse, and, of course, the luminous city of Paris, with its respected opera houses and the mighty Louvre offering a plethora of opportunities for cultural enrichment.

   Doing as the French do is only slightly more complicated than learning their language and embracing some of their many never-ending customs. One fine day, start with strong coffee and a croissant—with a buttery flaky body that tastes as good as one

PRECEDING OVERLEAF: *A sparkling gathering of twentieth-century pottery, flatware, stemware, and linens charm a family happy to be together.* OPPOSITE: *Resplendent with rich walnut paneling, a library layered with detailing assuredly casts its own light on European culture with help from the French Empire chandelier (circa 1850) that highlights the acanthus-leaf moldings and soaring ceiling. Over the mantel hangs an important painting from La Belle Époque, while Vervloet-Faes hardware from Belgium and a pale Aubusson area rug from Stark Carpet add further sophistication. Chenille curtains embellished with flanges and gimp hang on iron rods and rings from Palmer Designs in San Diego. Chic buttons made from the same gimp are set beneath the tacked top header.*

sold in a Parisian *boulangerie*—then read on, disregarding any plans for the morning.

The French believe:

You are what you know. In a country that embraces diplomas and where even three-year-olds *must* attend class, education lies somewhere near the very heart of French identity. This means that it is important to have a deep knowledge of France, a far-reaching view of the world, and opinions about a broad array of issues that can readily be articulated.

The French, as a class, are well-informed rather than stuck on the headlines of *Le Monde, Le Figero, Libération,* or any of the country's approximately seventy-five daily newspapers representing a wide range of beliefs. The popular *France-Soir* was founded as an underground paper during the German occupation of France in World War II, and it brought home some hard truths.

While delighting in onion soup and an unhurried *salade niçoise* at one of the countless cafes that in summer spill out onto the sidewalks, a person might eavesdrop on those expounding on everything from the economy to politics to their philosophy of life—all topics that can often evoke much emotion.

Assuming the language poses no problems, one can also get an earful about work stoppages (*grève,* or strike), if she or he strains to understand those passionately explaining their positions. When it comes to demonstrations, few countries can match France for frequency. But then, "How can you expect any kind of agreement from Frenchmen in a country where there are 270 different kinds of cheese?" asked General Charles de Gaulle after he was elected president of the Fifth Republic.

Staking claim to the air space over the great room shown on page 81 is an iron chandelier from France (circa 1870), happened upon at Marvin Alexander, Inc., in New York City.

With its massive limestone fireplace, distressed, wide-plank walnut floors, Aubusson area rug, and palette of rich earth tones—bark, moss, and terra-cotta—the décor is très château. Sofas tout Christopher Norman chenille chairs in a custom-colored Bennison that picks up the hues of the Travers plaid adorning the ottoman. All upholstery is from the Cameron Collection in Dallas.

Good manners are critical to the texture of France. With inbred courtesy and lives more gracious and less hurried than our own, the French exhibit refined old-fashioned manners when dealing with each other. In daily life, their conduct suggests a deep sense of respect and caring. Significance is attached to a warm welcoming handshake and the greeting ritual of placing a sincere kiss twice on each cheek. Filling the air with kisses is considered a social blunder.

It is also unimaginably rude for children to call their elders by any other than their surnames and proper titles. Unlike Americans, the French have no difficulty drawing the line of familiarity, since the ways they address one another reflect how well they know each other. Whereas most Americans use familiar first names too soon after meeting and readily shorten the names of others without being invited to do so, the French mark distances and underline social differences with the formal *vous* (you). The more familiar *tu* (you) is reserved for family and closest friends.

Trained in the forms of *politesse*, they also think twice about letting their children misbehave in public, and rule out other liberties that might be disturbing to others. Even cell-phone etiquette has unwritten rules, including not carrying on loud public conversations. While our addiction to cell-phone communication is all too audible in restaurants, airports, and even in streets, they have strict guidelines in consideration for others. Most are the product of common sense and everyday thoughtfulness, offering a respite from the irritations of ongoing ringing, intermittent static, and incessant chatter.

It is, for example, considered bad manners to call anyone after 9:30 P.M. or to phone a business associate at home on Saturday unless the person is also a close friend. To avoid intruding on relationships, the tactful only call family members and closest friends on Sunday.

Wealth and discretion go hand in hand. Equating elegance with restraint, the French deliberately avoid material indulgences that are outward measures of success. Although they have a propensity for quality goods, most frown on anything that appears extreme. For them, comfort and tastefulness are paramount, not high-priced luxuries or extravagant ways.

Despite Louis XIV's passion for the magnificently roomy Palace of Versailles and the remarkable blue Hope diamond, owning big homes, flawless jewels, and showy cars simply does not appeal to the sensibilities of moneyed French aristocrats. Heaven forbid that they should even think of renting F.A.O. Schwartz in Manhattan for a child's pajama party or installing a backyard ice-skating rink that turns into a basketball court in spring. For that matter, patronizing a produce store that offers valet parking would also be bad form, as would other American comforts more opulent than they could imagine. But then, ostentatious behavior is rare at every level of society, including among people of modest means with the confidence to do as they please.

Recoiling against living lavishly—a virtue deeply embedded in French culture—most Parisians live in modest but

Like a chic Pashmina shawl adding warmth and beauty, unexpected colors wrap this stunning lit à baldaquin *—canopy bed—custom made by Niermann Weeks.*

What better place to build fond childhood memories than in a make-believe kitchen set to delight? The tile with fleur-de-lis is really trompe l'oeil, hand painted on a terra-cotta Brunschwig & Fils wall covering. Inspired by the eighteenth-century painters who engaged in this lighthearted technique, San Francisco decorative artist Annette Etchevarry playfully brightened the stove, refrigerator—most everything in sight. Manuel Canovas fabrics trim the chair and ottoman.

nicely appointed apartment buildings, some that have been in the same family for generations, all in firm possession of graceful architecture and historic charm.

In general, the older the building, the more prestigious it is. Yet, as if a breach of good taste, this is not something residents would point out any more than high-end antiques dealers would divulge the names of those with the means and refinement to buy fine furnishings.

Frankly, nobody ever talks publicly about social standing or wealth; there especially seems to be an unwritten taboo against flaunting the latter. Regarding the former: the French are more apt to judge each other by their good taste (*bon goût*) or lack of it. Instead, net worth is a private affair, and the French consider themselves keepers of a tradition to be guarded as fiercely as the family jewels, making discretion treasured.

Aversion to public disputes about money runs deep in polite society. For example, restaurant tabs are controversy-free. Separate ones are for American tourists only. Rarely do we see the French awkwardly dividing a bill, though they may quietly split the tab away from curious eyes.

Even when the air is crisp, this playroom offers a magically sunny spot fit for a tea party with friends. With a white picket fence, rolling fields, and a tree that looks as if it would welcome climbing, a site designed for fun appeals to the child in each of us.

Most anytime is the right time to serve fine wines. Actually, lunch and dinner are often hours-long multicourse affairs, where vintage wines flow in a rapid stream and are as special and as well thought out as the food. With a taste for the good life and wine inherent to the dining tradition, it is only fitting that the French are adroit at wine-and-cheese-inspired pairings and also capable of using an extensive wine vocabulary confidently. For their part, enjoying a glass of an elegant Chardonnay, appreciating an expensive Bordeaux, or serving the most esteemed Champagne is worthy of conversation much like a special occasion about which they speak knowingly.

Knowingly or not, the French consume more wine than any other people—more than sixteen gallons a person annually, according to *Impact*, a trade publication. By comparison, Americans drink less than two gallons each.

Regardless, the former are particular about what they drink, believing the best wines emerge from deep, musty, cobwebbed cellars in France rather than sleek American wineries. Our wines have failed to penetrate the French market. By common consent, it seems the French maintain an all-consuming loyalty to their own, making no apologies for snubbing even excellent American wines, because to serve them would undoubtedly invite gossip and criticism.

Wine has some new competitors. To quench France's growing thirst for bottled water, supermarkets now showcase nearly forty types of mineral water, many from springs that cradle within the rugged Alps. Suddenly, too, there are more *salons de thé* (tearooms) dotting Paris than London.

Handcrafted tiles with lush vines in relief (standing out from the surface) bring the charm of French and Italian vineyards to an otherwise plain niche. Fittingly, the word tile *is rooted in the Latin verb* tegere, *meaning "to cover." Houston artist Ellen Santa Maria designed and produced the hand-thrown custom tiles shown here.*

After long days in the office, a person might crave the wide plains of Africa, or clearly a change of place for taking care of business. This room presents an argument for working in comfort at home—with tiger chenille window treatments, leopard-spotted carpet, and an antique partner's desk topped with hand-tooled leather. The desk was acquired from Frenchman Bruno de la Croix-Vaubois, whose store, Country French Interiors, is on Slocum Street in Dallas's design district. Aged leather finished with nail heads bestow dignity on writers' chairs from Ralph Lauren. Today's thirst for leather dates back to the 1920s, when Parisian designer Jean-Michel Frank first obtained leather from the revered Hermès for use in furniture making.

Tea became a fashionable beverage during the reign of Louis XIV, when he was advised to drink steaming cups for digestive reasons. These days, most every Parisian has a favorite tearoom as a preferred place to meet, devour fancy *pâtisseries*, and gossip—sparked by the glossy *Paris Match*.

With its marble-topped tables, huge mirrors, gilt-framed murals, and Napoleon III columns, no tearoom may be more enticing than the famously resplendent Angélina's at 226 rue de Rivoli, an easy walk from the Jardin des Tuileries in Paris's First Arrondissement (the French equivalent of zip codes). When Angélina's opened in 1903, it was christened Rumpelmayer, and soon began drawing stylish crowds. Coco Chanel, the undisputed leader of fashionable society, and novelist Marcel Proust are said to have once been among the countless others arriving *le five o'clock*.

August is the nation's decreed vacation month. Logical or not, the entire country shuts down at the height of summer for *les grandes vacances*, leaving hordes of tourists to fend for themselves in deserted cities and towns. Some suggest not traveling to France in the summer, and especially during August when the French flee to the Mediterranean. But this is precisely when there are hundreds of festivals across the regions and thousands of events that bask in the public's attention, which may explain why more than 80 percent of the French forego far-flung vacations in favor of spending their holidays in *la bella France*.

There are benefits to rest and relaxation. Shrugging off any criticism, the French allow themselves a freedom about the way they live their lives. To their way of thinking, it is critical to take their minds off intricacies of the day and simply idle for a while, even if this means indulging in a short after-lunch nap as Napoleon often did. As a result, they keep a close eye on the clock—and days come to a standstill at midday when the lengthy *pose midi* means that most small shops are closed between noon and two—and sometimes three—o'clock in the afternoon.

Though those on holiday often fail to appreciate the lull at a time when every minute counts, studies suggesting that brief naps renew energy, reduce errors, and increase productivity are routinely trumpeted in French papers. As proof that the rest of the world is coming around to their way of thinking, they report that some American companies, including Levi Strauss and Ben & Jerry's Homemade Inc., are trying out nap rooms with reclining chairs, blankets, and alarm clocks.

Inarguably, this kitchen owes a generous helping of its charm to the admirable tile marching up walls and hugging countertops. With its cabinets resembling mismatched pieces of furniture, it is impeccably suited to the taste of a cook who revels in creating classic dishes that are as pleasing to the eye as to the palate. OPPOSITE: *An antique commode is given a new life with exquisite Sherle Wagner fittings, while a necklace of fleur-de-lis, the heraldic symbol of unity and harmony in France, embraces the powder-room sink. The vintage mirror and the classic light fixtures also are worthy of the setting.*

Once tightly woven ticking was the traditional covering for French mattresses stuffed with cotton and horsehair, and the stripes hid imperfections in the weave. Nowadays, however, the fabric is no longer bedridden. Rather, it traverses everything from upholstery to lamp shades. The fabrics shown here are from Carlton V. A loved Wheaton terrier, loyal to the family who owns him, can easily be mistaken for the sea-grass carpeting.

A nineteenth-century iron stove with bright brass trim serves as a night table, catering to those with le bon goût *(good taste). It was acquired from Ainsworth-Noah in Atlanta. With standardized beds straggling into decorative history, finding antique beds that fit today's mattresses is nearly impossible. The queen bed shown here is from Charles P. Rogers in New York.*

IT IS FAIR TO SAY THAT NOWHERE ARE DOGS MORE INDULGED, CODDLED, OR PAMPERED.

Days should be filled with hobbies one is passionate about. With the newly instituted thirty-five-hour workweek giving everyone more leisure time, the French have discovered a passion for everything from games to gardening, from throwing pottery to painting to taking spelling (*dictée*) tests. Millions work on their spelling skills daily, though a poll taken by the décor specialist Castorama reveals that *le bricolage* (home improvement) is the favorite free-time activity. It ranks up there with spending time with family and pets, which still place above all else.

Dogs peek into our souls, accepting us as we are, charming us into feeling loved, protected, and joyful. As if lighting up lives were not enough, they are there at every turn, they listen when no one else seems to care, and they never let slip some inner truth. In return, the French lavish love and attention on their pets in ways that elicit human waves of envy. It is fair to say that nowhere are dogs more indulged, coddled, or pampered.

Believing that looking good on the outside is tantamount to feeling good on the inside, the French fill dog days with must-have treatments for the entire body at hand-picked places. Not only are they fussy about where *le chien* is regularly shampooed, fluffed, and manicured, but also they won't settle for bookings at anywhere less than the best day care and animal therapist. By all appearances, some humans do not have as impeccably tailored wardrobes.

Purebred or of uncertain origin, a posh pooch living in the lap of luxury can dart in and out of art galleries, boutiques, the cinema, and even expensive restaurants where menus feature special meals for their set. Fact is, some pet-friendly hotels boast twenty-four-hour room service for animals. Others, like Paris's legendary Hôtel Ritz, welcome dogs with open arms, special porcelain water bowls, and comfortable wicker beds dressed with custom-made blue blankets inscribed "I am Ritzy."

Not to be outdone, wicker beds made up with Italian linens await pets at the Pierre Hôtel in New York, and the Hôtel Plaza Athénée provides fluffy dog bathrobes. At the Mansion on Turtle Creek in Dallas, gourmet snacks and costly mineral water arrive in Waterford crystal bowls, while at Loews L'Enfant Plaza Hotel in Washington, D.C., "Fido's Filet" is served on a silver platter. But even rooms with splendid views of these major cities may hardly be worth putting up with the staid nightlife—something dogs would never dream of having in France. In America, most spend their evenings in, since pets are not permitted in restaurants.

In Paris, when *petit caniche* isn't feeling up to par, an owner can rest easy knowing that veterinary clinics will answer emergency calls with speeding ambulances fully equipped with oxygen tanks. Equally important, top dog sitters take their roles seriously, charging more than babysitters. However, the French are not known to deal with overpriced dog walkers.

Improbably enough, the top dog of choice is not the French poodle. It ranks after the German shepherd, which is thought most apt at fending off menacing intruders, thus addressing the French fear for safety. To a slightly lesser degree cocker spaniels, Labradors, and golden retrievers have captured French hearts, but the love for them is no less serious than other breeds.

Fine writing paper is an expression of one's good taste and attitude, while a handwritten note is the nicest way to express appreciation. In most circles, E-mail and Post-Its are a bit too informal for communicating with friends and colleagues. Instead, the French typically gravitate toward thick, creamy, high-quality writing sheets designed to punctuate births and marriages, express condolences, and respond to invitations begging for attention.

Dedicated to the practice of writing letters, a stationery wardrobe often consists of many different papers, some monogrammed and others colored. Most importantly, letter writing is not only for women. As soon as French children are old enough to stay up past eight, gifts require thoughtful thank-you notes to aunts, uncles, and grandparents.

Those with unerring good taste would never dream of entertaining formally without creating a glamorous sense of

Alluring toiles de Jouy prints originated in the French town of Jouy-en-Josas, near Versailles, in the 1770s. Traditionally printed on white or linen ground with but one other color used for the design, toiles traveled to the States after the American Revolution. Though Americans still use them more sparingly than the French, we commonly mix them with solids, stripes, and checks—most always staying within the same color family. The sophisticated polished-steel canopy bed became a French classic after being introduced around 1760. This one is from Shannon & Jeal in San Francisco.

occasion. Tables overflow with fine china, crystal, bevel-edged place cards, and crisp linen napkins, providing the perfect backdrop for meals designed to please the senses as much as the palate. Heavy silver flatware with the tines of the fork turned toward the tablecloth draw attention to the family initials as highly polished serving pieces and candelabras with tall tapers reflect the setting's light.

Hallmarks on French silver usually indicate the district where a piece was made, and the control marks bespeak the year it was produced. Sterling in France is marked with the symbol of Minerva being clobbered. Some pieces also bear the maker's personal stamp.

Vintage linens are one of life's greatest treasures. However, while ferreting out the old, high-quality new linens do not fail to catch French eyes. As a result, an entire room may be devoted to meticulously embroidered bed and table linens, quilts, and dishcloths sometimes tied with ribbons. More often, they, along with pillows and towels, are stored behind hand-carved doors in scented armoires, where the great mix with the good after being impeccably folded.

With a deep affection for fresh linens, the French care for their riches by using gentle washing compounds, line drying, and carefully hand pressing.

Although there are no hard-and-fast rules for bed linens to qualify as truly sensual, the most elegant ones do have some common traits. All are white or ecru, and rashly expen-sive, of course, but other than being 100-percent cotton or linen, the French prefer not getting caught up in thread count, which they say can be misleading. (There is a difference, of course, between 120 and 250 threads per inch, but beyond that they insist thread count doesn't really matter. As a result, in Europe, thread count is rarely mentioned.)

Instead, there is a consciousness of how linens feel when touched, the comfort they offer, and their embellishments— embroidery, appliqué, and applied laces. For their beds, Europeans seek high grades of Egyptian or pima cotton and a soft finishing process, with lace trim, hemstitching, or hand-embroidered edges.

Without a doubt, Paris is the *haut monde* of final resting places. Anyone who dies in Paris can be buried in one of the city's fifteen *cimetières*, but the truth is, a good spot is sometimes hard to find. Dearly departed foreigners receive less than a warm reception at the most-prized address. At Pére-Lachaise only the most well-connected French dead can rest in splendor. But Montparnasse is also a fashionable burial ground in the vicinity. Also, as you might expect, there is a lavish cemetery exclusively for canine companions. Established in 1899, La Cimetière des Chiens is on the edge of Paris.

Bed linens with never-ending beauty have been lovingly pressed then carefully stacked and stored in this eighteenth-century Louis XV walnut armoire festooned with garlands. The intricately carved flower-basket cartouche shamelessly grabs attention; however, the exquisite pierce-carved apron also elicits awe since it required even more skill to produce. Inessa Stewart Antiques is a direct importer of eighteenth- and nineteenth-century French armoires and other vintage pieces.

FOREIGN AFFAIRS

❧

"The truth is found when men are free to pursue it."
— FRANKLIN DELANO ROOSEVELT

One might get the impression that the French approve of nearly anything as long as it is done with style, yet every day they do things that seem inappropriate to us.   Though it may seem strange, the French feel no shame in their office flirtations, two-hour lunches, or public smoking. They even look indulgently upon the sexual indiscretions of their leaders. And though American health experts warn against the hazards of dining late in the day and eating too much red meat or high-fat foods, they snub our dietary guidelines. Dazzled by portions rich and flavorful, they obviously see no reason to change. After all, statistics show the French suffer fewer health problems than Americans. Also, the rate of obesity in America is about three times that of France, a fact they are quick to point out.   As a rule, even when dieting, the French eat and drink well. This means partaking of plenty of fruits and vegetables, replacing butter with olive and

PRECEDING OVERLEAF: *Prized copper pots, admirable tile, and a commercial range keenly evoke an enthusiasm for cooking in this beautifully garnished French-inspired kitchen. The sink overlooks interesting planters and urns spilling over with foliage onto well-tended grounds.* OPPOSITE: *Before ascending a graceful pecan staircase with wrought-iron railing, light bounces freely off the limestone floor and a stone pot filled with a mound of hydrangeas.*

colza oils, swapping natural fructose for processed sugar, dishing up fish every other day, and drinking wine daily, since grapes—especially their seeds—are reportedly rich in antioxidants.

While nothing irritates the French more than being dismissed rather than accepted as helpful critics, they deny resenting American suggestions or at least do not express such feelings to foreigners. In truth, French feelings about the United States, Americans, and any ideas that are offered in friendship have always been decidedly mixed.

By most counts, the French have long viewed Americans with a *soupçon* of mistrust, in part because they see an ongoing volley between our modern ideas, which they view as a menace to their culture and their traditional convictions. While ideas age quickly in the States, perhaps because we tend to take more risks, throughout history the French have been more interested in re-creating the past.

In the not-so-distant past, the American press has chided the French for being too rigid, since changes tend to creep into their lifestyles slowly, if at all.

With inbred resistance to shedding old habits, they are prone to do things a certain way just because that is the way they have always been done. Often, it seems as if they are stuck in time. Only half a century ago, for example, for the French to owe money was considered almost criminal and to pay by check unusual.

Whereas, it was once the deployment of American nuclear missiles that caused alarm, it is now McDonald's fast-food chains (viewed as a symbol of industrialized agriculture), Coca-Cola™, genetically modified crops (grown from seeds implanted with genes of other living organisms), and hormone-treated beef that have stirred a new round of concern lately, despite American assurances that they are safe.

With an old-fashioned chalkboard that helps to create familiar warmth, this breakfast room unabashedly pretends to be a bistro, where, anchored by top French wines, one artful plate after another arrives at the table in a parade of flavors, colors, and textures. To clear up any confusion, a brasserie—the French word for "brewery"—is generally noisy and bursting with spirit, while a bistro tends to be cozier and more intimate. These days, neither is quite as thick with smoke. Though the seventeen million smokers who reside in France represent approximately 35 percent of the population, recent polls reveal one in five are either trying to kick the habit or plan to do so soon.

Shapely rush-seat armchairs imported from Italy surround a 72-inch-round Portuguese dining table from Michael Taylor Designs, San Francisco. In this breakfast room, lords, ladies, and children sit as equals just as kings and knights did long ago. Interestingly, it was not until 1944 that French women were given the right to vote. Since 1945, however, the statue of the woman Marianne, the French version of Uncle Sam, has graced public buildings, symbolizing the spirit of liberty, equality, and brotherhood in France.

The soft colors favored by Madame de Pompadour, whose example was followed by all of Europe's privileged class, swathe this guest room in the comforts of her private world—a choice of pillows, an elegant writing table, a reading chair (unseen), even lavender with its aromatic properties. Here, the pièce de résistance is the French headboard. During the eighteenth century, it served as an overdoor.

But some say the far greater issue is French sensitivity to American power. Despite many shared interests, plus being the world's oldest allies, France and the United States are seemingly always squabbling over something. As a result, they have been called the "prickliest pair." On September 1, 1999, new policy centers designed to ease future tension opened in Washington and Paris.

Vintage Fortuny fabrics exude a serene tone in a sanctuary with comforting richness. Donna Burley at Straight Stitch fabricated the elegantly detailed soft furnishings, proving that fine workmanship does not go unnoticed. The wall covering is from Brunschwig and Fils.

PARLEZ-VOUS FRANÇAIS?

"Genuine hospitality…
cannot be
described, but it is
immediately felt."
— HECTOR GUIMARD

Ever since Thomas Jefferson lived in Paris just steps from the Champs-Élysées, Americans have been eagerly following in his footsteps, exploring, enjoying, and confirming the reputation of *Ville Lumière* as one of the world's most beautiful cities. ❧ While much has changed in past centuries, old-fashioned street lamps still cast dancing pools of light on the city's splendid buildings and famous wide boulevards that have long been a haven for writers, musicians, artists, and intellectuals filled with aspirations. ❧ To this day, the City of Light plays host to more than three million Americans annually. In addition, France is now the world's top tourist destination with more than 70 mil-

PRECEDING OVERLEAF: *The rough-and-cut limestone facade of this stately home with strong Gothic roots captures the ambiance and allure of old-world France while respecting today's American lifestyle. Richly embellishing the exterior is a soaring slate roof. The formal courtyard and porte cochere add to its grandeur.* OPPOSITE: *Plush pillows with imperial trimmings sit at the foot of a bed that is steeped in history.*

lion visitors each year. (Spain is second in luring seasoned travelers; the United States, third, according to the French Ministry of Tourism.) Her people, however, have long been widely criticized for seldom making travelers feel welcome. ❧ Some years ago, French society earned a

For a breathtaking view of Paris, ride the funicular or climb the steps to the Basilique du Sacré Coeur atop Montmartre, Paris's tallest hill at 425 feet. With its gleaming onion-shaped dome, it is one of the city's most recognized sights.

reputation for being curt and standoffish toward Americans. As our interest in France unfolded, their resistance to English grew. The clerks in many shops appeared proper enough, yet with a trying silence and chilly demeanor, they openly shunned English-speaking customers, making it clear that they preferred paltry French with a Texas or New York accent to no French at all.

Stubbornly refusing to speak English even when, in the minds of some, they could have capably done so at the first sign of confusion, they instead pretended not to comprehend. Word got around that it was their protest against the rudeness they saw in American society invading France, along with a feisty amusement at unabashed displays of American showiness.

Shopping the Avenue Montaigne, Paris's equivalent of New York's Madison Avenue, lined with such European

This pewter lavabo *(washstand) has little to be humble about. Unearthed at the flea market at Clignancourt, its fluting is markedly Parisian.*

Satisfying a passion for fine details, proper proportion, and an obsession with quality, boldly scaled light fixtures—with the knowing spirit of those keeping watch over the Place Vendôme—fittingly garb this sprawling stone facade. The winsome fixtures by Murray's Iron Works in Los Angeles reflect brilliant craftsmanship.

fashion boutiques as Chanel, Louis Vuitton, and Valentino, we helped reinforce their images in our own inimitable way by demonstrating shopping at its extravagant best, frequently appearing to take excess to excess.

Beyond the French almost-smug good taste, however, they also tarnished their image by raising well-groomed eyebrows at Britons—supposedly because of the latters' penchant for serving fish and chips in *plastic* baskets. But it is more likely that in French minds there is a lingering belief that British food simply doesn't measure up when compared to French cuisine.

In unguarded moments, they even acknowledged their *très français* snobbery toward fit and chic Italians, whose tastefully decorated rooms, innovative regional gastronomy,

A low stone wall displays the address of the home at the end of the courtyard. In France, sapphire blue plaques with white numerals often reveal addresses, too.

and thought-provoking beauty rival their own but who fail to fall for the superiority of the French—and like the Britons are neither pleased, amused, nor intimidated by the French people's haughty, off-putting ways.

There are signs the French are mellowing, however slowly. If not due to France's surging popularity as a tourist magnet, perhaps it is a concession to her fickle economy that is prompting her people to become increasingly accepting of outsiders in hopes of continuing financially certain times ahead.

Most likely, though, it is that the young have trouble working up the requisite animosity toward the United States. Having moved past the clichés that were formed a generation ago, some of France's sharpest young minds are now seeking their fortunes outside the country.

One cannot deny that a massive wave of young well-educated French professionals from the best schools are fleeing France for the United States and London financial districts. As their parents struggle to understand the departure from decades-old attitudes, as well as the new vistas of choice, those who come of age in this new era are hoping also to improve their English language skills, which in their minds are a prerequisite for success.

With lessons to be learned, it is probably wise for us to start brushing up on our French, or better yet, mastering those frustrating irregular verbs. Why? Because chances are that we, too, may soon be headed for the French capital, where the museums, shops, even the 379 Métro stations can act as a classroom for an American bent on speaking French.

AS THEIR PARENTS STRUGGLE TO UNDERSTAND THE DEPARTURE FROM DECADES-OLD ATTITUDES, AS WELL AS THE NEW VISTAS OF CHOICE, THOSE WHO COME OF AGE IN THIS NEW ERA ARE HOPING ALSO TO IMPROVE THEIR ENGLISH LANGUAGE SKILLS, WHICH IN THEIR MINDS ARE A PREREQUISITE FOR SUCCESS.

To escape the summer heat, terra-cotta pots hug the rail leading to a garage apartment.

A painted desk and an upholstered chair turn a bedroom into a boudoir, or lady's private room, providing a quiet spot to be alone or, if one so chooses, to receive and entertain guests. Although the boudoir was at the center of the royal court during the reign of Louis XV, the word is actually French for "place to pout or sulk," so a boudoir is not merely a matter of looks; attitude counts, too. Here, a Kenneth Meyer ribbon trim drips from the sumptuous but subtle Christopher Norman silk plaid.

Savoir Faire

"Proper words in proper places, make the true definition of style."
—Jonathan Swift

France not only has a staggering number of stylish places to dine—some pricey—but also a wealth of affordable bistros, smart cafes, and neighborhood brasseries, where no reservations are taken and tables fill up fast. Relishing an elegant meal, good wine, and interesting conversation in a spot that is overrun with American tourists, though, has long been unappealing to the French, who famously linger over meals. ❧ Fashionable establishments do play host to vacationing Americans; however, typical *maître* or *maîtres d'hôtel* simply shy away from seating a steady stream of American patrons at once. As a result, reservations can be especially hard to come by at trendy restaurants where the food is as fancy as the price. And getting in may take some doing, including calling more than a few weeks in advance plus reconfirming, then reconfirming once again. ❧ As everywhere, chic spots reward regulars with cushy banquettes or the best tables and comfortable

PRECEDING OVERLEAF: *It is said that "the torch of love is lit in the kitchen," and it may very well be true as this chef enjoys preparing healthy meals that gently foster her family's eating habits meant to last a lifetime. Unlike Americans, the French drench most food in* beurre, *or butter, sniffing at our dietary guidelines with the same disdain they reserve for an indifferent wine. Pretty lace curtains commonly screen kitchen windows both here and abroad.* OPPOSITE: *A centuries-old fireplace transported from France serves not only as the centerpiece of this posh breakfast room but also as a monument to the country's bond between architecture, beauty, and haute cuisine. The antler chandelier is old, as are the high-backed chairs and the farm table mellowed with age.*

upholstered chairs located in the front of the restaurant beside the windows. But tourists are often steered to the handful of less-pleasant places with straight-backed chairs and hard seats near the kitchen, in a plant grove, or in remote areas far from the main dining room, where they are out of sight.

Service may be a further affront. Affable waiters who hover with friendly professionalism around the French can be less than welcoming toward strangers on holiday. Of course, some servers are cordial, helpful, and attentive even toward Americans who offend their sensibilities by sampling another's *pâte de foie gras*, *magret de canard* (breast of duck), or *crème brûlée*, a habit the French think rather distasteful. (The American practice of sharing food or, less politely, spearing a morsel off someone else's plate is also a pet peeve of Letitia Baldrige, the well-known etiquette expert.) Other *garçons* make it pointedly clear—by intentionally neglecting to offer bread, serve mineral water, or even pour the wine—that some tables may not be worth their attention.

Beneath all this is resentment against those not fluent in French, fed partly by the fear that foreigners will not fully appreciate the way cuisine expresses the culture of France and sets it apart from other European nations. Presumably, then, those from other countries will fail to notice the artful manner in which each course is arranged on the plate, though it adds another dimension to the culinary pleasure.

In restaurants with plush crimson seating, the presentation is unreservedly theatrical, including both the excitement and drama of a Broadway show that produces breathlessness in the audience as the curtain rises. With grand entrances, flurries of activity, and electricity filling the air, dining rooms become center stages as casts, hungry for acclaim, showcase their talents with plates fit for the critics and fleeting moments of promise for those seated in the pathway to selected tables.

For help in coming up with added storage space, this American need not bother asking a Parisian who lives in a prewar apartment with outdated kitchen. Everyday dishes stack conveniently on the open shelves of a rack once used in a boulangerie for displaying gorgeous lemon meringue, banana cream, and pecan pies as well as chocolate tortes and freshly baked macarons *(macaroons).*

Fessing up to an infatuation with red, the late Parisian designer Vincent Fourcade once said, "A room without red is like a woman without lipstick." Of course, color preferences are purely personal since not everyone perceives light the same way. But color can affect one's world in both positive and negative ways. Red reportedly appeals to the palate.

Even so, some waiters can be overheard openly criticizing Americans for routinely leaving their knives and forks at all different angles rather than putting them together on the plate to show that they are finished. Not incidentally, the French also grudgingly claim Americans are unaware that in France servers are afforded a measure of respectability.

Fortunately, most kitchens operate in happy worlds of their own, turning out dishes that help keep the French in everyone's good graces, thus avoiding leaving sensitive Americans simmering over various affronts.

Taking novelist Alexandre Dumas at his word, Americans remain ever mindful that an ongoing appreciation for French food is at the heart of the country's culture. Hand-textured walls, color washed in taupe, add layers of age, becoming a distinctive podium for the stenciled saying that reads "An omelet is to cuisine as a sonnet is to poetry." A cellar with an enviable collection of carefully chosen wines is but a few feet away. Its impressive door was hand-forged by Frenchman Max Brun, whose talent is a legacy from his father, his homeland, and a French college. He now has a workshop in Bloomfield, Colorado.

In the classic French kitchen, old copper pans sway conveniently from pot racks within arm's reach, and most everything—familiar bowls, pastry trays, wineglasses, and faïence—is lined up on open shelves rather than sandwiched into cupboards. (With no disrespect for the French, more than a few Americans yearn for more order, which is to say they favor fitted cabinets with pull-out compartments where there is a place for everything and everything can be hidden in its place. Then a commercial range and stove hood spice things up by becoming the focus.) Travertine stone, a remnant of the eleventh century, is available through Country Floors in New York as well as showrooms nationwide.

FRENCH
INFLUENCES

*"That which we elect
to surround ourselves with
becomes the museum
of our soul and the archive
of our experiences."*

—THOMAS JEFFERSON

To many people, French furniture is a status symbol of sorts, with its broad stylistic range reflecting the glory of the ages. Among this worldly clique of sophisticated people, there are a strong respect and a keen demand for furnishings that hearken back to the past, defining the fashionable French lifestyle. For them, the search for majestic wood pieces is a pursuit of passion. Yet in healthy economic times the French are less inclined to part with their antiques; so fewer armoires, commodes, and tables come into the market, and those that do appear sell quickly. The not-so-secret truth is that French furniture has a loyal following in the United States, but by no means are we alone in our devotion. With eighteenth-century pieces thought of as the height of elegance, buyers as far away as Egypt, Saudi Arabia, Turkey, and South America are also frenzied fans. Of course, the French decorative arts can take many forms. During much of the baroque

PRECEDING OVERLEAF: *Bathed in tradition dating back to the ancient Greeks and Romans, a soothing and restful bain de salle (bathroom) captures an old-world feeling with its spirit of nobility. The freestanding marble soaking tub is carved from one solid piece of marble, and the heated floor is set in twenty-four-inch squares.* OPPOSITE: *With ironwork worthy of French craftsmen, doors that once graced an eighteenth-century chateau and a treasure of French accents—standards of excellence set long ago—still flourish in this entry.*

period (1643 to 1715), Louis XIV, the Sun King, ruled France from the glorious Palace of Versailles. In keeping with his extravagant image and the upward spiral of opulence that followed in the *Régence* era from 1700 to 1730, connoisseurs of eighteenth-century grandeur marry nobly carved wooden pieces with sophisticated tapestries, shimmering brocades, and regally tasseled velvets, though perhaps none more assiduously than certain Europeans.

Passionate about exquisite things that lend an air of romance, Parisians frequently swirl in seductive silks, whispering sheers, and sensuous chairs from the more beguiling rococo period (1730 to 1760), when Louis XV and his mistress Madame de Pompadour had great influence on the decorative arts.

Others in Paris prefer to live with neoclassical, the style of Louis XVI, who was overthrown during the French Revolution. But not everyone is sold on the trappings of splendor. Elbowing them aside, those of varied tastes and means living outside the French capital find joy in an eclectic mix of periods that overlap. And although some New York limestone apartments are indeed bedazzling, Americans typically favor a more understated elegance, fully aware that our so-called twenty-first-century French-country rooms often do not bear even a passing resemblance to early interiors with their rag rugs, dried flowers, handmade quilts, and rooster prints.

A generation ago, it was common for early pieces with simplistic beauty to find faithful audiences in those who saw themselves as caretakers of bygone eras. But now that rural ways of life have nearly vanished, there is even wider approval for more refined furnishings, sometimes kilometers from French-country's primitive past.

Of course, nothing is more wondrous than a baby, but could anything be as special as a christening gown handed down through the generations? This distinctive one, framed behind glass, can easily be admired from the entry.

OTHERS IN PARIS PREFER TO LIVE WITH NEOCLASSICAL, THE STYLE OF LOUIS XVI, WHO WAS OVERTHROWN DURING THE FRENCH REVOLUTION.

An antique commode set against a dramatic black wall covering gives an unassuming powder room a strong presence in a very sophisticated French way. Like the classic black dress, noir *is forever in vogue. But here it takes traditional French-country design to new heights.*

Bolts of soft, flowing verde Haas *taffeta—hand loomed in Italy—create sweeping bed and window treatments with a European air. But France has its own bed culture that pays little mind to other parts of the continent. Topping the mattress is a stuffed and quilted mattress pad; next come two flat sheets then a blanket with sheets covering both sides. A goose-down duvet supplies the final layer. The lavender plaid sheer is from Clarence House. On an opposite wall hangs an old black-and-white map of Paris with its rues, avenues, boulevards, and allées framed in sections.*

While correctly associating French country with unassuming splendor, we have taken it upon ourselves to come up with our own version of this look that is not only a style but also an attitude and a way of life.

Of course, there is no single way to live or even to decorate. With a foundation of self-expression, our rooms are disarming repositories for an ever-evolving blend of furnishings that indulge stylistic preferences. To be sure, some purists like to stay under the same king when furnishing a room; others are more daring in their choices, mixing periods and styles without sweeping aside all signs of modern life. But left to our own devices, we inextricably link elegance with grace and living graciously in settings redolent with history.

The fact is, in redefining French country, we are not afraid to make a statement. With American flair and a decidedly French air, our rooms are discreetly chic.

A custom-painted Patina chest and bed have all the makings of family heirlooms, while the Bennison linen floral woven in England adds warmth. Reserving its charm for the young lady who snuggles in the beauty of this room is a sugar-britches tuffet from Plenty's Horn. The scalloped matelassé blanket cover hides a modest box spring.

Kay Thompson's hyperactive Eloise, who orders from room service, rides elevators, and roams the halls of New York City's Plaza Hotel where she lives, would undoubtedly cast an approving eye on this bathroom with a pedestal sink. To indulge those with sophisticated tastes, the tile, fittings, and fixtures are available through Waterworks, headquartered in Danbury, Connecticut.

With every little girl's fantasy to be a princess, obviously a little royal treatment was in order when it came to furnishing this room. An extra-deep pillow-top mattress and a duvet plumped with the finest down are piled á la The Princess and the Pea, though it is doubtful this fair-haired charmer will even feel the pea once tucked in the regal Farmhouse bed that is sure to become a cherished part of her heritage. Not to worry. A chair from Plenty's Horn in Pittsburg, Texas, appears appropriately majestic with smocking and shirring. And dreams come alive as birds on a line look down from their preferred perch.

FRENCH TWISTS

*"Modern man associates
himself with the ancient
world, not ... to reflect,
like a mirror, but to
capture its spirit and apply
it in a modern way."*
— PALLADIO

Pulling together a room awash in chic French trappings, not to mention both twenty-first-century sensibility and old-world sophistication, takes a bit of courage. Though any designer would tell you that a room is, quite simply, the sum of its indispensable parts, it can be daunting figuring out which parts to choose, let alone selecting from a plethora of options. ∞ It would be foolish, of course, to try meticulously listing the pieces needed to create the perfect harmony, since spaces are as varied as the people who use them. Besides, there are several different approaches to artfully packaging interiors. ∞ The famed decorator Billy Baldwin once said,

"Never forget that a room starts from the rug up," but most any piece can offer inspiration, including an exquisitely painted bed or an antique picked up at the famed

PRECEDING OVERLEAF: *Bringing the elegance of bygone times into a new era are vintage leather trunks that not only serve as a coffee table but also offer a reminder that, at one time, getting there was half the fun. In these fashionable quarters for visiting in-laws, glowing Summer Hill Ltd. upholstery and fabrics express the true meaning of warmth.* OPPOSITE: *Exuding the cherished worn look of the antiques that inspired them, this individually handcrafted and hand-finished bed and desk from The Farmhouse Collection in Hailey, Idaho, is rooted in the south of France. Charming, too, in its simplicity is the hand-painted vase. This gift from a precious granddaughter reminds her proud nana to stop and give the Gypsy Curiosa roses (from Ecuador) more than a moment's glance.*

Marché aux Puces, the vast weekend flea market on the outskirts of Paris. ∞ Some ideas are more unlikely than other sources of

inspiration, such as an old French stove or a vintage medical-supply cabinet. Then, too, something that is a seemingly random acquisition (for example, an Aubusson throw pillow that started life as a carpet) can turn out to be a stepping-stone to a promising room.

Actually, some American designers take Billy Baldwin's words of advice to heart. Others let a favorite fabric dictate the palette of a room. Still others permit light or the absence of it to shape the way they decorate a space. Seasoned designers know that protocol dictates only that colors must flow from one room to the next without boring repetition.

Although the French believe in living in beautifully created spaces, their rooms are to be enjoyed as well as admired. Drawing upon their country's own extraordinary history, they determinedly tie together past centuries, focusing on dreams without compromising matters of taste and need.

At best, rooms provide a snapshot of lifestyles while balancing the spirits of comfort and calm, allowing everyone—family, friends, and pets—to experience their pleasures. As the French see it, a devotion to children and pets does not mean one should sacrifice decorating or that some living spaces should be out of bounds. From an early age, children are taught to respect fine furnishings, and good manners are a must.

Obsessed with their pets, the French treat their canine companions like children, though, by all appearances, French children must follow more rigid rules. Interestingly, they view American children as having no limits, no manners, no set bed-times, and parents who bow to their every demand. Not shy about critiquing our offspring or offering pointed opinions, they profess to be markedly unimpressed by how children behave on the western side of the Atlantic.

Designed to hold most everything a girl needs is a hand-painted chest that is new. But it might very well be a legacy of a past generation's thoughtfulness or an old possession revived with ingenuity and paint for very little money. Dated frames were tinted white; those new are from The Wicker Garden in New York City.

AS THE FRENCH SEE IT, A DEVOTION TO CHILDREN AND PETS DOES NOT MEAN ONE SHOULD SACRIFICE DECORATING OR THAT SOME LIVING SPACES SHOULD BE OUT OF BOUNDS.

Worthy of a beautiful baby, the hand-painted Jane Keltner bed is a charming mix of sweet floral fabrics from Travers and Manuel Canovas. Carefree sea-grass carpeting runs underfoot. As appropriate for today as for tomorrow is the painting by Suzanne Etienne, represented by the McRae-Hinckley Showroom in San Francisco.

Living graciously calls for generously scaled furnishings that embrace the finest France has to offer. An eighteenth-century Aubusson tapestry has been inset in the ottoman. The table is also eighteenth century, and the velvet photo album was found in Eze.

But with pets having the run of houses, forgiving fabrics and floor coverings are often important considerations. As a result, humble slipcovers that can be washed or dry-cleaned often protect sofas, chairs, and ottomans with luxurious fabrics and impressive detailing hidden underneath. To their credit, the French also camouflage weary furniture, giving pieces a fresh look far less expensively than replacing or reupholstering.

Still, there are no magic formulas for giving a room a French twist other than cleverly moving beyond the expected, and certainly never underestimating French pride. Whether one lives in a trophy house, a charming farmhouse, or a cramped apartment, he or she can introduce a bit of France by engaging his or her artsy side.

The truth is, a person no longer need be "to the château born" to live as if he or she were. Rows of leather-tooled books spilling from shelves and a few glimpses of a former French life (not to worry if it is someone else's) can make someone feel as if he or she owned a pied-à-terre in Paris's pricey Eighth Arrondissement.

After all, "You are a King by your own fireside, as much as any Monarch on his throne," Cervantes once said. Impossible, Americans reply. "*Impossible*. The word is not French," pointed out Napoleon.

Portuguese tile and les accessories of French and Italian descent that have outlived their original use add more than a dash of charm while bestowing an international flavor on this country kitchen.

With its aristocratic good looks conjuring up rich images of old-world splendor, this room begs for an eclectic gathering worthy of the setting. Replete with glistening silver and a breathtaking chandelier, all that is missing are white-gloved waiters faithful to the tradition of formal lingering French dining. The dining room was not commonplace in American homes until the mid-nineteenth century. OPPOSITE: The furnishings in this handsome family room honor Louis XV with Corragio Textiles dressing up the sofas and Bailey & Griffin adorning the chairs. Curtains are Brunschwig & Fils embellished with a Schumacher trim. Like all fashionable rooms, this one is rich in antiques.

FRENCH ACCENTS

*"Go confidently in the
direction of your dreams.
Live the life
you have imagined."*

—HENRY DAVID THOREAU

The following suggestions may help you think like the French.

The past must be ever present. In France, history and tradition abound, so it is only fitting that the French revel in their country's breathtaking beauty while striving to keep alive a taste for the life that was. Little wonder, then, that they are collectors second to none. Clusters of family portraits are the backdrop for *objets de charme* — cherished boxes, interesting clocks, candlesticks, *faïence* (fine glazed ceramics), and other vintage finds rescued from flea markets. Clignancourt and Porte de Vanves are among their favorite Parisian haunts. This is not to say that rooms stray toward the fussy or the cluttered. If anything, there is awareness that more is *not* always better. One generously scaled accessory rather than many smaller ones is often seen highlighting a

PRECEDING OVERLEAF: A grouping of faïence over this breakfast-room window is sure to capture even the most casual observer's attention. The old-world charm of Paris makes its famous flea markets one of the best places to hunt for interesting plates and other unusual pieces. OPPOSITE: Nostalgia for the simple ways of one's ancestors is the hallmark of a French-country design; so, not surprisingly, an array of distinctive accents often rescued from an obscure past garnish American countertops.

spot. True clutter (for example, magazines) is relegated to baskets.

Nonetheless, assembling and artistically grouping related

Despite the aristocratic scale of the furniture, this game room reaches out to the young with a less-than-serious sense of play. A Wurlitzer jukebox and an antique billiard table stand ready to introduce the fun life.

small items together in a seemingly effortless way is a trait at which the French excel. Though hardly short of perfection, rooms do not exude a staged or studied look nor do they appear overly thought out. Rather, accessories appear to have offhandedly found their own way to their locations. Only those who know how particular the French are realize that nothing is ever left to chance, which may explain why they spend a lifetime searching for finishing touches worthy of their rooms.

A setting that gives the impression it has evolved over time adds luster to its image. As large houses throughout France have given way to less spacious ones with smaller rooms, many people find that past generations are happily represented among the bazaar of antiques furnishing their homes. Never mind that these legacies might be somewhat

A doctor may have ordered the antique medical cabinet filled with supplies. But there is no need to wonder what the designer had in mind when she came up with the idea for a wall covering splattered with trunks, suitcases, and mini LXVs. Though the French have a way of intimidating, they can also inspire vacationing at the Le Grand-Hôtel du Cap-Ferrat overlooking the Mediterranean Sea. The hand-printed wallpaper is available to the trade only through Peter Fasano.

overwhelming for less-roomy new settings. Interiors are defined around them.

Furthermore, it matters not if guests must sit on a potpourri of mismatched chairs. Contrary to what many people may think, it is the feeling of harmony that is important rather than sameness.

French-country interiors call for furnishings that are imposing since this is the scale the eye is accustomed to seeing. Putting boldly scaled, dignified old wood pieces in their proper place can be challenging, however. Unless the right pieces find their way to the right spots, their attention-grabbing presence can disturbingly slant the visual weight to one side of a room. Balance, not symmetry, is the secret behind successful settings.

Le salon (sitting room) envelops the family's most treasured, though not necessarily most expensive, furniture and *objets d'art*. With a loyalty to the French national flag and to the hand-me-downs from family, rooms exude a friendly aura suited to everyday life.

Of course, no one piece of furniture or accessory can create a defining look. But you could call the armoire the quintessential French-country piece. Europeans have long relied on it as a sensible essential, gifted in bringing both beauty and welcome storage space to living rooms and bedrooms.

Clearly, nothing could be finer than an armoire with deep carving, a shaped top, and the patina of age to anchor a setting with its quiet grandeur. But the French offer no apologies for one with unadorned surfaces. Though it may hardly be the sort of which dreams are made, there is an appreciation for a vintage piece to which only they have access. The fact is, sentimental value often makes it even more special.

A roomful of new matching furniture lacks character. Blatantly turning their backs on new and shiny wood pieces, the French say that more than a few costly armoires, commodes, and writing tables simply do not measure up to the antiques that hail from France. For them, proof lies squarely by comparing a reproduction to an original. Indeed, faithful furniture not only requires painstaking design but also relies on old-world craftsmanship to burnish pieces sheenless. A reproduction is destined to become a family heirloom only when knowledgeable people wonder if it is an antique.

Fine painted furniture, regally finished, had its beginnings in China about thirty-five hundred years ago. But its legacy lingers at the Farmhouse Collection in Hailey, Idaho. The tea-washed Bennison linen floral, from an early document, is artfully fashioned so it appears to have aged over time. Birdcages were gathered in France.

Quality counts. With beauty in astonishingly handsome carvings and with luxury hidden in the springs or the fabric adorning a rolled arm, there are valid reasons some generously scaled sofas, chairs, and wood pieces are more expensive than others. Though it is hard to resist a bargain, the French generally shun temptation and buy the best they can afford instead.

THOUGH IT IS HARD TO RESIST A BARGAIN, THE FRENCH GENERALLY SHUN TEMPTATION AND BUY THE BEST THEY CAN AFFORD INSTEAD.

Capturing the romance of the late-eighteenth century is a récamier, inspired by the French painter Jacques-Louis David's Portrait of Madame Récamier, *which hangs among the Louvre's 33,765 works of art. Napoleon exiled the provocative Parisian madame in 1805, but she returned to the city after his defeat at Waterloo in 1815 and resumed her salon. The charming painted table is from a French flea market.*

Far from anything goes, being French means a certain predisposition for a sense of proportion and a discerning eye. It also requires a way of thinking, living, and decorating, where the latter mirrors those who live in the home. And, indeed, this is how a sumptuous master bath sated with antique nickel fixtures and objets d'art came to epitomize style.

A regal master bedroom with polished pecan floors, curtains that are works of art, and legendary Fortuny fabrics, reads Paris, but any formality is offset with a sense of relaxed sophistication. In 1240, Henry III of England commissioned the first king-sized bed, an unforgettable lit à colonnes, or four-poster, with painted canopy and heavy curtains that not only protected him from draughts but also screened him from those passing through his chambers, as privacy was nonexistent.

Humble sea grass, jute, and coir signal an easygoing mood, lessening the seriousness of spaces. Sisal resists spots and stains, and looks terrific bound with linen; however, water can discolor some sisal. While many French people pre-fer bare floors, some are drawn to the beauty of hand-loomed orientals that warm settings with color and texture. Mostly, however, there is a preference for lovingly worn *Savonneries*, which were once woven for royalty, and precious old Aubussons with their tapestry-like weave. Always they lounge in rooms with minimal traffic.

In French bathrooms, where the palette rarely strays from the neutrals, scented sea salts, washcloth mitts, and soft, fresh towels stacked neatly on chairs are not enough to bathe one in luxury. Jostling for space are pedestal sinks in lieu of built-in vanities or washstands with shiny tubular legs, marble-slab tops, and under-counter mounted porcelain basins. Those with nickel fittings are more easily maintained than brass. Well-lit beveled mirrors in wide classic frames give even small spaces more presence. As if further proving that small touches do make a difference, mirrors are seldom glued to the wall. OPPOSITE: *It has been said that toile de Jouy is the fabric that best represents La République Française. Marie Antoinette enveloped her Versailles boudoir with a toile while her husband Louis XVI bestowed royal supplier status on the Oberkampf factory in Jouy-en-Josas in the Paris suburbs.*

Details distinguish rooms. Masters of detail, the French have a knack for making the ordinary seem precious. Vintage or not, they hand-paint everything—chests, chairs, tables, and tiles—with amazing creativity.

Applying their inventive spirits, the French fashion rooms with fabric-covered walls and, almost as an afterthought, flourishes of papers. Some spaces brim with a mélange of mirrors, others with trompe l'oeil landscapes or columns. With or without trimmings, or *la passementerie*— fringes, tassels, cording, tie-backs, tapes, and braids—curtains hang as luxuriously as couture gowns and are as beautifully made. The French do not skimp on fabric, so settings look instantly richer. Revealing an inviting mix of patterns and textures that complement each other, fabrics also dictate moods.

Furniture floats instead of stiffly hugging the perimeter of walls. There are fires in fireplaces, throws on most every chair, and decorative pillows to rest against. Most eye-catching of all are the animal prints used as accents in measured amounts.

The French have a way of capturing light so that it creates the romantic mood of Paris's diagonal avenues. The key is in the layering of candles, sconces, picture lights, and carefully placed table and floor lamps with low-wattage bulbs. They shun track lighting, believing it can be jarring as well as unforgiving in casting shadows on the face.

Always there are sprays of fresh flowers either straight from the garden or from local markets, restoring spirits with the pleasure they deliver. For some, monochromatic blooms arranged en masse are the epitome of quiet elegance. Others delight in loose and airy dramatic waves of color.

What could be more welcoming than bedding from Italian linen maker Frette, unless it is these exquisitely shirred bumper pads and pretty crib skirt fabricated by Donna Burley at Straight Stitch in Dallas? Together they cradle baby with love. OPPOSITE: *With lions, zebras, and elephants in J. Robert Scott's monochromatic toile marching across the upholstered walls, there is no mistaking that this dazzling nursery is for the youngest family member. The hand-smocked, diamond-patterned curtain heading reflects Susan Chastain's meticulous attention to detail in her San Francisco workroom. Bathing the room in soft light is a nineteenth-century alabaster chandelier (unseen) that hangs overhead. The bee, adopted by Napoleon, symbolizes the goddess of love in mythology.*

GARDEN GRANDEUR

∞

*"The logic of nature
is impeccable."*

— HECTOR GUIMARD

In France, an invisible bridge is evident between the house and garden. Bringing the outside in and transporting the inside out is far from an afterthought. ✵ Like a landscape painting, flower beds, potted plants, and garden benches are carefully placed, defining outdoor spaces with help from cast-iron gates that are as decorative as they are functional. Inside, lush palettes of cut flowers, fabrics, and wall coverings couple with a banquet of classical shapes and textures—wood, stone, sisal—paying homage to nature's serene beauty and doubling as a stylish venue for those who live and entertain in the home. ✵ And yet, no matter how carefully planned a home's interior may be or how tailored a room to its inhabitants' needs, no décor can top the outdoors' inherent beauty. With woodland paths, spiraling topiary mazes, and a variety of plantings, the famous resplendent gardens of Versailles, which are visited by more than

PRECEDING OVERLEAF: *A shady recess of branches shares property rights with clusters of plants and flowers, creating a gracious outdoor room, or arbor, where there was none. With roots in the sixteenth century, mirrors multiply the growth, allowing everyone seated around the table to enjoy the garden in the distance.* OPPOSITE: *Gardening is having its moment in the sun as its popularity continues to grow in both the United States and France. A potting room that opens onto the yard signals that here, however, the flowering interest is more than a passing fancy. An old cupboard fitted with a drain is reserved for arranging blooms. Books abound. Cuttings from the past were gleaned at the* Marché aux Puces, *the flea market of the Porte de Vanves that is open only on weekends.*

In the south of France, blue is the prevailing hue, so it naturally has an overpowering allure—reminding us of the sea, painted shutters, and a way of life that includes the pleasures of dining al fresco in Provence. The French, like people in other Mediterranean countries, put great store in the color blue, believing it can keep all manner of misfortune away and spurn insects in a region where screens are rarely used on windows or doors. Thirty-five percent of Americans also say it is their favorite color, according to the Pantone Color Institute in New Jersey, which forecasts design-industry trends. OPPOSITE: *A love affair with all things French blossoms in this quiet spot away from the pressures of the world. The generously scaled furnishings gracefully weather the elements while the Louis XV fountain, a remnant of the past, offers a fitting backdrop for enjoying friends and catching a breath of fresh air.*

ten million people annually, still inspire both great French artists and modern-day gardeners.

Despite hostile piercing winters, the French Revolution, and two world wars, the gardens flourished until hurricane-force winds roared across parts of Europe over the Christmas holidays in 1999, felling millions of trees, including more than 10,000 on the grounds of the seventeenth-century palace. Many of them were more than a hundred years old. According to meticulous records, Marie Antoinette's much-loved Virginia tulip tree, planted in 1783, lay in the debris, as did a Corsican pine, planted in 1810, which honored Napoleon. Both will be replaced.

But inspiration comes, too, from the placid life in the French countryside with its winding roads, brooks, ponds, and rows of hedges that explode in a burst of blossoms during the summer. In a country where the weather varies greatly from region to region—even as spring meanders into summer—the climate and soil make gardening no easy task.

Looking like a page from a storybook, this enchanting two-story playhouse complements a stately Louis XV stucco main house that reflects the ambiance and allure of old-world France.

In a garden that is undeniably French, yet is set under the American sun, a cake made of hydrangea shares the spotlight with a fine champagne.

Designers' Notebook

∞

*"Have nothing in your
houses which you do
not know to be
useful or believe to be
beautiful."*

—William Morris

For interior designers and decorators, there is no such thing as one-stop shopping for fabrics, furniture, antiques, or upholstery.

Aside from combing showrooms in design centers (based in major metropolitan areas) where hundreds of lines are represented, we are regular visitors to well-known department stores such as Neiman Marcus, Bergdorf Goodman, Barneys New York, Bloomingdale's, and Saks Fifth Avenue. Also among our favorite stomping grounds are the retail establishments of Pierre Deux, Ralph Lauren, Crate & Barrel, Pottery Barn, Pier 1 Imports, Williams-Sonoma, and Banana Republic. Then, too, we are big believers in catalog shopping with Ballard Designs and Horchow, definitely worth a second look. *More of our favorite resources are:*

PRECEDING OVERLEAF: Billowing white sheers, flirting with the open air, whirl among Anna French's warm saturated hues in a young girl's room awash with details that delight the eye. The French open their windows even when it is chilly, believing that sluggishness results from central heating with its stale air. OPPOSITE: *At this side entrance, dated iron gates lead to a terrace where a child may delight in the novelty of feeding the fish. A small French fountain is the centerpiece of the peaceful shallow pond.*

ANTIQUE FURNISHINGS
AND ACCESSORIES

Jacqueline Adams
2300 Peachtree Road NW
Suite B 110
Atlanta, GA 30309
Tel. 404.355.8123

Agostino Antiques Ltd.
808 Broadway
at 11th Street
New York, NY 10003
Tel. 212.533.3355

Nick Brock, Antiques
2909 North Henderson
    Street
Dallas, TX 75206
Tel. 214.828.0624

Country French Interiors
1428 Slocum Street
Dallas, TX 75207
Tel. 214.747.4700

Fireside Antiques
14007 Perkins Road
Baton Rouge, LA 70810
Tel. 225.752.9565
www.firesideantiques.com

Charles Gaylord Antiques
2151 Powell Street
San Francisco, CA 94133
Tel. 415.392.6085

The Gray Door
1809 West Gray Street
Houston, TX 77019
Tel. 713.521.9085

Ed Hardy San Francisco, Inc.
188 Henry Adams Street
San Francisco, CA 94103
Tel. 415.626.6300
www.edhardysf.com

Joyce Horn Antiques
1008 Wirt Road
Houston, TX 77055
Tel. 713.688.0507

Junque
2303 A Dunlavy Street
Houston, TX 77006
Tel. 713.529.2177

The Lotus Collection
445 Jackson Street
San Francisco, CA 94111
Tel. 415.398.8115

The Mews
1708 Market Center
    Boulevard
Dallas, TX 75207
Tel. 214.748.9070

Joseph Minton Antiques
1410 Slocum Street
Dallas, TX 75207
Tel. 214.744.3111

Made In France
2912 Ferndale Place
Houston, TX 77098
Tel. 713.529.7949

Carl Moore Antiques
1610 Bissonnet Street
Houston, TX 77005
Tel. 713.524.2502

Jane Moore Interiors
2922 Virginia Street
Houston, TX 77098
Tel. 713.526.6113

A subtle palette gives this private fitness center the look of a luxurious spa with help from a mirror that magnifies the space. Though far from pretentious, there is a Frenchness to the décor, with walls striped and glazed—methodically brushed with four values of restful dove gray. Taking their cue from the plump robes that follow rubdowns, windows are wrapped in white terry from Rogers & Goffigon threaded tight through grommets. Coffee sisal sweeps the floor. A massage room, steam shower, sauna, and hot tub are just steps away.

Orion Antique Importers,
    Inc.
1435 Slocum Street
Dallas, TX 75207
Tel. 214.748.1177

John Rosselli
523 East 73rd Street
New York, NY 10021
Tel. 212.772.2137
    and
255 East 72nd Street
New York, NY 10012
Tel. 212.737.2252

Inessa Stewart Antiques
8630 Perkins Road
Baton Rouge, LA 70810
Tel. 225.769.9363
    and
5201 West Lovers Lane
Dallas, TX 75209
Tel. 214.366.2660

Brian Stringer Antiques
2031 West Alabama
Houston, TX 77006
Tel. 713.526.7380

The Gables
711 Miami Circle
Atlanta, GA 30324
Tel. 404.231.0734
www.thegables.com

Uncommon Market, Inc.
2701 Fairmount
Dallas, TX 75201
Tel. 214.871.2775

Watkins, Schatte, Culver,
    Gardner
2308 Bissonnet Street
Houston, TX 77005
Tel. 713.529.0597

BATH FITTINGS

Czech & Speake
350 - 11th Street
Hoboken, NJ 07030
Tel. 800.632.4165
www.homeportfolio.com

Kallista, Inc.
2446 Verna Court
San Leandro, CA 94577
Tel. 888.4.Kallista
www.kallistainc.com

St. Thomas Creations, Inc.
1022 West 24th Street,
    Suite 125
National City, CA 91950
Tel. 619.474.9490
www.stthomascreations.com

Sherle Wagner, International
60 East 57th Street
New York, NY 10022
Tel. 212.758.3300
www.sherlewagner.com

Waterworks
60 Backus Avenue
Danbury, CT 06810
Tel. 203.546.6000
www.waterworks.com

Freshly splashed with color, Anna French wall covering and fabric create a charming bathroom.

CARPETS

Asmara, INC.
451 D Street
Boston, MA 02210
Tel. 800.451.7240
www.asmarainc.com

Design Materials
241 South 55th Street
Kansas City, KS 66106
Tel. 913.342.9796

Mark, Inc.
323 Railroad Avenue
Greenwich, CT 06830
Tel. 203.861.0110
www.brunschwig.com

Rosecore Carpet Co., Inc.
D&D Building
979 Third Avenue
New York, NY 10022
Tel. 212.421.7272
www.rosecore.com

Stark Carpet
D & D Building
979 Third Avenue
New York, NY 10022
Tel. 212.752.9000
www.starkcarpetcorp.com

DECORATIVE HARDWARE

E. R. Butler & Co., Inc.
Maison J. Vervloeot-Faces
75 Spring Street, 5th Floor
New York, NY 10012
Tel. 212.925.3565
www.erbutler.com

P. E. Guerin, Inc.
21–23 Jane Street
New York, NY 10014
Tel. 212.243.5270
www.p.e.guerin.aol.com

Nanz Custom Hardware
20 Vandam Street
New York, NY 10013
Tel. 212.367.7000
www.nanz.com

Palmer Designs
7875 Convoy Court, Suite 5
San Diego, CA 92111
Tel. 858.576.1350
www.palmer-design.com

FABRICS AND WALL COVERINGS

Anna French
Classic Revivals
One Design Center Place
Suite 534
Boston, MA 02210
Tel. 617.574.9030

Bennison Fabrics
76 Greene Street
New York, NY 10012
Tel. 212.941.1212

Brunschwig & Fils
75 Virginia Road
North White Plains,
   NY 10603
Tel. 914.684.5800
www.brunschwig.com

Manuel Canovas
111 Eighth Avenue, Suite 930
New York, NY 10011
Tel. 212.647.6900

Carlton V
D & D Building
979 Third Avenue, 15th Floor
New York, NY 10022
Tel. 212.355.4525

Clarence House
211 East 58th Street
New York, NY 10022
Tel. 212.752.2890
www.clarencehouse.com

Rose Cummin
Fine Arts Building
232 East 59th Street, 5th Floor
New York, NY 10022
Tel. 212.758.0844

Coraggio Textiles
1750 - 132nd Avenue NE
Bellevue, WA 98005
Tel. 425.462.0035
www.coraggio.com

Nancy Corzine
256 West Ivy Avenue
Inglewood, CA 90302
Tel. 310.672.6775

Cowtan & Tout
111 Eighth Avenue, Suite 930
New York, NY 10011
Tel. 212.647.6900

Elizabeth Dow, Ltd.
155 Sixth Avenue, 4th Floor
New York, NY 10013
Tel. 212.219.8822
www.edowltd.aol.com

Peter Fasano
964 South Main Street
Great Barrington, MA 01230
Tel. 413.528.6872

Fortuny, Inc.
D&D Building
979 Third Avenue, 16th Floor
New York, NY 10022
Tel. 212.753.7153
www.fortunyonline.com

Pierre Frey, Inc.
12 East 33rd Street
New York, NY 10016
Tel. 212.213.3099

Haas
50 Dey Street
Building One
Jersey City, NJ 07306
Tel. 201.792.5959

Hinson & Company
2735 Jackson Avenue
Long Island City, NY 11101
Tel. 718.482.1100

Marvic Textiles
50 West 91st Street, Suite 4
New York, NY 10024
Tel. 212.362.8288

Quadrille
50 Dey Street, Building One
Jersey City, NJ 07306
Tel. 201.792.5959

Nobilis
57-A Industrial Road
Berkeley Heights, NJ 07922
Tel. 908.464.1177
www.nobilis.fr

Christopher Norman Inc
41 West 25th Street,
  10th Floor
New York, NY 10010
Tel. 212.647.0303
www.christophernorman.com

Osborne & Little
90 Commerce Road
Stamford, CT 06902
Tel. 203.359.1500

J. Robert Scott
500 North Oak Street
Inglewood, CA 90302
Tel. 310.680.4300
www.jrobertscott.com

Rogers & Goffigon
41 Chestnut Street
Greenwich, CT 06830
Tel. 203.532.8068

Scalamandré
300 Trade Zone Drive
Ronkonkoma, NY 11779
Tel. 631.467.8800

F. Schumacher Compay
79 Madison Avenue,
  14th Floor
New York, NY 10016
Tel. 212.213.7900
www.fschumacher.com

Jim Thompson
1694 Chantilly Drive
Atlanta, GA 30324
Tel. 404.325.5004
www.jimthompson.com/branch.
html

Travers
504 East 74th Street
New York, NY 10021
Tel. 212.772.2778
www.traversinc.com

The ottoman of today is an upholstered seat or bench with neither a back nor arms, only vaguely reminiscent of the long backless settee from which the privileged sultan of the vast Ottoman Empire ruled during the fourteenth century. Regardless, this descendant remains heir to the ottoman name. (The Ottoman Empire ended in 1922; the next year, Turkey became a republic.)

FURNITURE

Charles P. Rogers
55 West 17th Street
New York, NY 10011
Tel. 212.675.4400
www.charlesprogers.com

Dennis & Leen
8734 Melrose Avenue
Los Angeles, CA 90069
Tel. 310.652.0855

The Farmhouse Collection, Inc.
PO Box 3089
Twin Falls, ID 83303
Tel. 208.736.8700

Hamilton, Inc.
8417 Melrose Place
Los Angeles, CA 90069
Tel. 323.655.9193

Jane Keltner
136 Cumberland Boulevard
Memphis, TN 38112
Tel. 901.458.7476
www.janekeltner.com

Niermann Weeks
Fine Arts Building
232 East 59th Street, 1st Floor
New York, NY 10022
Tel. 212.319.7979

Old Timber Table Company
908 Dragon Street
Dallas, TX 75207
Tel. 214.761.1882

Patina, Inc.
351 Peachtree Hills Avenue, NE
Atlanta, GA 30304
Tel. 404.233.1085
www.patinainc.com

Plenty's Horn
15 County Road 2210
Pittsburg, TX 75686
Tel. 903.856.3609

Shannon & Jeal
722 Steiner Street
San Francisco, CA 94117
Tel. 415.563.2727

Summer Hill, Ltd
2682 Middlefield Road
Redwood City, CA 94063
Tel. 650.363.2600

Michael Taylor
1500 Seventeenth Street
San Francisco, CA 94107
Tel. 415.558.9940

GARDEN ORNAMENTS

Elizabeth Street Garden
  & Gallery
1172 Second Avenue
New York, NY 10021
Tel. 212.644.6969

Lexington Gardens
1011 Lexington Avenue
New York, NY 10021
Tel. 212.861.4390

Proler Oeggerli
2611 Worthington Street
Dallas, TX 75204
Tel. 214.871.2233

Treillage, Ltd.
418 East 75th Street
New York, NY 10021
Tel. 212.535.2288

IRON WORK

Brun Metal Crafts, Inc.
2791 Industrial Lane
Bloomfield, CO 80020
Tel. 303.466.2513

Ironies
2222 Fifth Street
Berkeley, CA 94710
Tel. 510.644.2100

Murray's Iron Work
5915 Blackwelder Street
Culver City, CA 90232
Tel. 310.839.7737

Potter Art
4500 North Central
  Expressway
Dallas, TX 75206
Tel. 214.821.1419
www.potterartmetal.com

LINENS

E. Braun & Co.
717 Madison Avenue
New York, NY 10021
Tel. 212.838.0650

Frette
799 Madison Avenue
New York, NY 10021
Tel. 212.988.5221

Léron Linens
750 Madison Avenue
New York, NY 10021
Tel. 212.249.3188

D. Porthault, Inc.
18 East 69th Street
New York, NY 10021
Tel. 212.688.1660

Pratesi
4344 Federal Drive, Suite 100
Greensboro, NC 27410
Tel. 336.299.7377

LIGHTING, LAMPS, AND CUSTOM LAMPSHADES

Marvin Alexander, Inc.
315 East 62nd Street
New York, NY 10021
Tel. 212.838.2320

Bella Shades
Bella Copia
255 Kansas Street
San Francisco, CA 94103
Tel. 415.255.0452

Chameleon
231 Lafayette Street
New York, NY 10012
Tel. 212.343.9197

Paul Ferrante, Inc.
8464 Melrose Place
Los Angeles, CA 90069
Tel. 323.653.4142

Ann Morris Antiques
239 East 60th Street
New York, NY 10022
Tel. 212.755.3308

Murray's Iron Work
5915 Blackwelder Street
Culver City, CA 90232
Tel. 310.839.7737

Nesle
151 East 57th Street
New York, NY 10022
Tel. 212.755.0515
www.dir-dd.com/nesle.html

Niermann Weeks
Fine Arts Building
232 East 59th Street, 1st Floor
New York, NY 10022
Tel. 212.319.7979

Acorns that venture beyond the usual put a playful spin on this elegantly shaped Versailles sofa —a work of art from the Cameron Collection at George Cameron Nash in Dallas. The handwoven area rug is from Stark Carpet.

Panache
719 North La Cienega
  Boulevard
Los Angeles, CA 90069
Tel. 310.652.5050

STONE AND TILE

Ann Sacks Tile & Stone
8120 NE 33rd Drive
Portland, OR 97211
Tel. 503.281.7751
www.annsacks.com

Country Floors
15 East 16th Street
New York, NY 10003
Tel. 212.627.8300
www.countryfloors.com

Paris Ceramics
151 Greenwich Avenue
Greenwich, CT 06830
Tel. 203.552.9658
www.parisceramics.com

Walker Zanger
8901 Bradley Avenue
Sun Valley, CA 91352
Tel. 818.504.0235
www.walkerzanger.com

TRIMMINGS AND *PASSEMENTERIE*

Kenneth Meyer Company
1504 Bryant Street, 3rd Floor
San Francisco, CA 94103
Tel. 415.861.0118

Leslie Hannon
  Custom Trimmings
4018 East 5th Street
Long Beach, CA 90814
Tel. 562.433.0161

Renaissance Ribbons
PO Box 699
Oregon House, CA 95961
Tel. 530.692.0842.
www.renaissanceribbons.com

West Coast Trimming Corp.
7100 Wilson Avenue
Los Angeles, CA 90001
Tel. 323.587.0701

Hugging the wall of a young girl's room is a nineteenth-century daybed that sits in the shadows of a ciel de lit, or free-hanging cupola. Both are dressed in matching Schumacher prints. The wisteria tumbling down walls adds fantasy, since seeing is not necessarily believing when it comes to trompe l'oeil.

DIRECTORY OF
INTERIOR DESIGNERS
AND FIRMS

Susan Arnold,
   Allied Member ASID
Susan Arnold, Inc.
2042 Utica Square
Tulsa, OK 74114
Tel. 918.584.7766
Fax. 918.587.4424

Deborah Fain, ASID
Deborah Fain & Associates
4241 Buena Vista Drive, Suite 5
Dallas, TX 75205
Tel. 214.521.9637
Fax. 214.521.9638

Beverly Heil,
  Allied Member ASID
Bev Heil & Associates
2905 North Henderson Street
Dallas, TX 75206
Tel. 214.220.2015
Fax. 214.220.0602

Patricia Herrington
P. DESIGNS
P.O. Box 1330
Vail, CO 81658
Tel. 970.926.5725
Fax. 970.926.5724

Rebecca Hughes
Rebecca T. Hughes Interiors
1520 Market Street
Galveston, TX 77550
Tel. 409.765.5933
Fax. 409.765.6028

Thomas Manche,
   Allied Member ASID
Tom Manche Interiors
7532 Cromwell Drive
Suite 1N
St. Louis, MO 63105
Tel. 314.727.3139
Fax. 314.727.9247

Joseph Minton, ASID
Joseph Minton Inc.
3320 West Seventh Street
Forth Worth, TX 76107
Tel. 817.332.3111
Fax. 817.429.6111

Betty Lou Phillips,
   ASID and IIDA
Interiors by BLP
4278 Bordeaux Avenue
Dallas, TX 75205
Telephone: 214.599.0191
Facsimile: 214.599.0192

Christina Phillips, ASID
CMP Designs
5001 River Bluff Drive
Fort Worth, TX 76132
Tel. 817.292.3994
Fax. 817.292.3694

Kelly Phillips,
   Allied Member ASID
Kelly Phillips Interiors
3604 Dorothy Lane
Fort Worth, TX 76107
Tel. 817.737.8281
Fax. 817.737.2439

Marilyn Phillips
Loren Interiors
1125 Riverbend Drive
Houston, TX 77063
Tel. 713.973.6475
Fax. 713.973.8859

Richard Trimble, ASID
Richard Trimble &
   Associates, Inc.
6517 Hillcrest Road,
   Suite 318
Dallas, TX 75205
Tel. 214.363.2283
Fax. 214.363.6364

DIRECTORY OF
ARCHITECTS

Richard Drummond Davis,
   Architect
4310 Westside Drive,
   Suite H
Dallas, TX 75209
Tel. 214.521.8763
Fax. 214.522.7674

Kurt Segerberg, Architect
Don Schieferecke, Architect
Segerberg & Mayhew
   Architects
1000 South Frontage
   Road West
Vail, CO 81657
Tel. 970.476.4433
Fax. 970.476.4608

Robbie Fusch, Architect
Fusch, Serold & Partners
5950 Berkshire Lane,
   Suite 1500
Dallas, TX 75225
Tel. 214.696.0152
Fax. 214.696.6938

PHOTOGRAPHIC CREDITS

Nancy Edwards: vi, vii, 1, 30, 31, 34, 36, 37, 54, 55, 58, 59, 60, and 176.

Emily Minton: endsheets, copyright page, 16, 17, 18, 19, 20, 21, 24, 25, 27, 29, 35, 41, 42, 43, 48, 49, 50, 51, 57, 61, 62, 63, 64, 65, 68, 70, 71, 72, 73, 74, 75, 79, 80, 81, 84, 86, 87, 88, 89, 90, 91, 93, 94, 99, 100, 101, 102, 103, 108, 109, 113, 114, 115, 118, 119, 120, 121, 122, 123, 125, 126, 127, 128, 129, 130, 131, 132, 133, 135, 136, 137, 138, 140, 141, 145, 146, 147, 148, 149, 150, 151, 153, 154, 155, 156, 157, 161, 164, 165, 168, 169, 171, 173, and back jacket.

Dan Piassick: front jacket, viii, x, 12, 13, 15, 23, 26, 28, 44, 45, 46, 47, 53, 67, 69, 76, 77, 82, 85, 96, 97, 107, 112, 117, 139, 142, 143, 152, 159, 160, 162, 163, 167, and 174.

Alise O'Brien: 52.

Russ Ohlson: author's photograph on back flap.

C. Thomas Studios: 33, 110, and 111.

James F. Wilson: title page, 38, 39, 104, and 105.

DESIGNER CREDITS

Susan Arnold, Allied Member ASID: 50, 126, 145, and 161.

Deborah Fain, ASID: 19, 64, 65, 89, 99, 102, 103, 114, 115, 118, 127, 141, 151, 164, 165, and 169.

Patricia Herrington: 119.

Beverly Heil, Allied Member ASID: front jacket, viii, 15, 23, 26, 28, 44, 45, 46, 47, 53, 69, 107, 117, 159, and 167.

Rebecca Hughes: 12, 13, 76, 77, 139, 142, 143, 152, and 160.

Thomas Manche, Allied Member ASID: 52.

Joseph Minton, Allied Member ASID: back jacket, 156, and 157.

Betty Lou Phillips, ASID: 17, 24, 29, 33, 35, 42, 43, 48, 49, 70, 71, 72, 75, 80, 81, 84, 87, 90, 91, 94, 100, 101, 110, 111, 113, 120, 121, 122, 123, 128, 129, 130, 132, 133, 135, 146, 147, 148, 149, 153, 154, 155, 162, 163, 168, 171, and 173.

Christina Phillips, ASID: 74, 93, 136, and 137.

Kelly Phillips, Allied Member ASID: 131.

Marilyn Phillips: copyright page, 51, 61, 62, 63, 74, 86, and 88.

Richard Trimble, ASID: 16, 18, 25, 27, 41, 67, 73, 82, 85, 96, 97, 109, 125, 138, 140, 150, and 174.

ARCHITECTURAL CREDITS

Richard Drummond Davis, Architect: title page, 38, 39, 104, and 105.

Robbie Fusch, Architect: front jacket, viii, x, 12, 13, 23, 26, 27, 28, 47, 112, and 117.

Kurt Segerberg and Don Schieferecke, Architects: 33, 35, 110, and 111.